Elite • 92

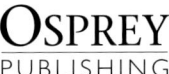

OSPREY
PUBLISHING

World War II Medal of Honor Recipients (1)

Navy & USMC

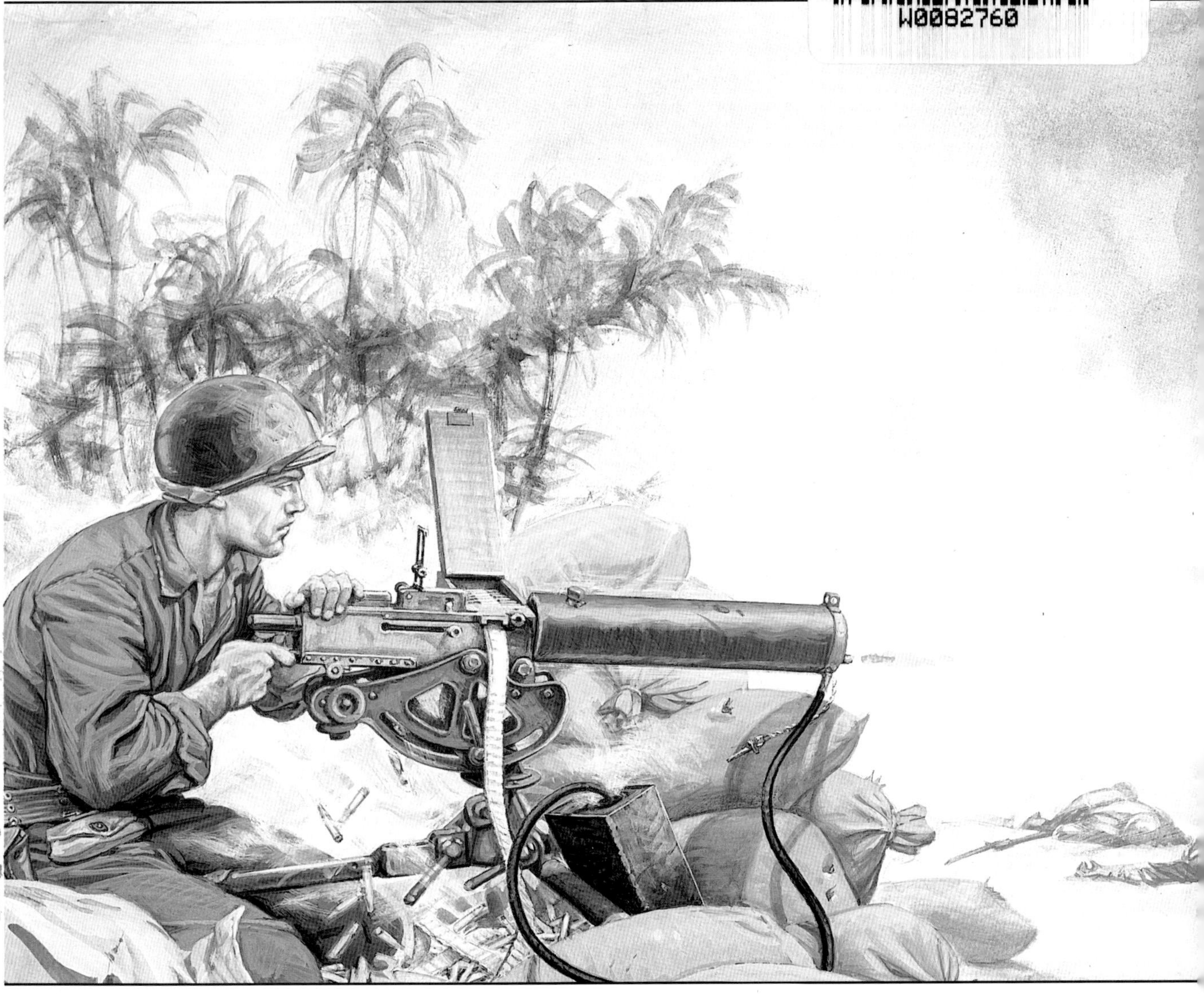

R Hargis & S Sinton • Illustrated by Ramiro Bujeiro

First published in Great Britain in 2003 by Osprey Publishing
Elms Court, Chapel Way, Botley, Oxford OX2 9LP, United Kingdom.
Email: info@ospreypublishing.com

© 2003 Osprey Publishing Ltd.

ISBN 1 84176 613 5

CONSULTANT EDITOR: Martin Windrow
Editor: Anita Hitchings
Design: Alan Hamp
Index by: Alan Thatcher
Originated by Electronic Page Company, Cwmbran, UK
Printed in China through World Print Ltd.

03 04 05 06   10 9 8 7 6 5 4 3 2 1

A CIP catalog record for this book is available from the British Library.

FOR A CATALOG OF ALL BOOKS PUBLISHED BY
OSPREY MILITARY AND AVIATION PLEASE CONTACT:
Osprey Direct UK
P.O. Box 140, Wellingborough, Northants, NN8 2FA, UK
E-mail: info@ospreydirect.co.uk

Osprey Direct USA
c/o MBI Publishing
P.O. Box 1, 729 Prospect Ave, Osceola, WI 54020, USA
E-mail: info@ospreydirectusa.com

www.ospreypublishing.com

Artist's note

Readers may care to note that the original paintings from which the color plates in this book were prepared are available for private sale. All reproduction copyright whatsoever is retained by the Publishers. All enquiries should be addressed to:

Ramiro Bujeiro, C.C.28, 1602 Florida, Argentina

The Publishers regret that they can enter into no correspondence upon this matter.

WORLD WAR II MEDAL OF HONOR RECIPIENTS (1) Navy and USMC

THE MEDAL OF HONOR

CONTROVERSY SURROUNDED THE IDEA of an award for military merit in the first century of United States history. In the minds of many, awards for military action belonged to the old European aristocratic order. Others, mindful of the difficulties and hardships of a soldier's life, saw the need for some recognition of bravery in war. The conflict between these differing opinions prevented the establishment of an award system for America's military for almost 90 years.

Those favoring military awards prevailed, but only for a while. George Washington, Horatio Gates, and John Paul Jones were given medals for their service in the Revolution. In 1782, Washington established an award for "any singularly meritorious action." This award took the form of a purple cloth heart, outlined with braid, to be worn on the uniform coat. This original Purple Heart, known as "The Badge of Military Merit" was limited severely in its award and only three awards are recorded. Soon after, the Purple Heart fell into disuse until 1932, when General Douglas MacArthur, then Army Chief of Staff, reincarnated it as an award for wounds received in combat.

Pictured is the original 1862 Medal of Honor awarded to USN personnel. This particular medal was awarded to Thomas Gehegan, a gun captain of the USS *Pinola*, for bravery during the Battle of New Orleans Bay. (US Navy)

In the period between the Revolution and the Civil War, there was effectively no official medal or device by which a soldier's bravery could be recognized. Only once during this period, at the time of the Mexican War of 1847, did the need for recognition of individual gallantry lead to the establishment of a "Certificate of Merit". This certificate, awarded to more than 500 men, entitled the recipient to two dollars per month extra pay, but did not provide for any medal or other insignia to indicate its award. Thus, the recipient remained anonymous to all but his immediate comrades.

Early in the Civil War, the Navy, perhaps recognizing that a difficult and arduous period lay ahead, established an award to recognize gallantry in the crisis. Congress passed Public Resolution 82 to establish a medal "to be bestowed upon such petty officers, seamen, landsmen, and marines as shall most distinguish themselves by their gallantry and other seamanlike qualities during the present war." On December 21, 1861, President Lincoln signed Public Resolution 82 into law establishing the Navy "Medal of Valor". Six months later, a similar award was authorized for the Army. At the height of the War in 1863, an unprecedented

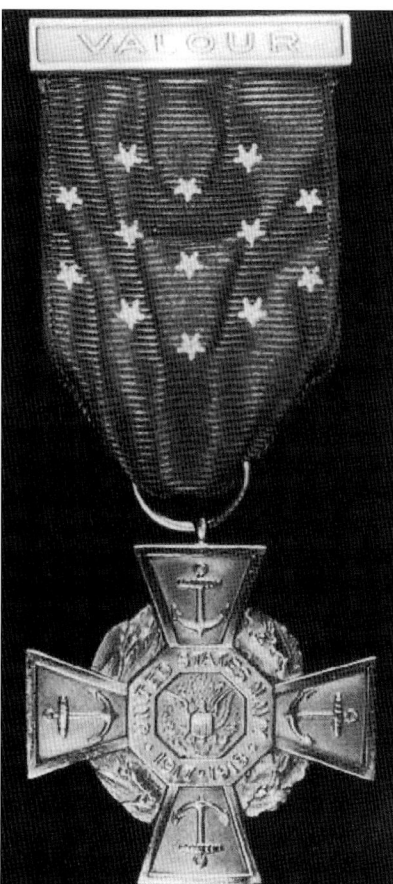

action took place: the award, known as the "Medal of Honor", was made a permanent decoration. Interestingly, while the Army authorized an award to officers and enlisted men by 1864, Navy and Marine Corps officers were not eligible for award of the medal until 1915.

The original medal was a bronze five-pointed star, two inches in height, supported by an anchor. In the center of the star Minerva stood, holding aloft a shield. To the right was Discord, a crouching figure, slinking off at the sight of Minerva. The entire central motif was surrounded by 34 stars. The ribbon was solid blue at the top and striped vertically with red and white at the lower end. In 1913, the ribbon was changed from red/white/blue to a solid light blue with 13 white stars woven into the ribbon. At each end of the ribbon were two metal rectangles: the upper one mounted on the back with a pin for attachment to the uniform; and the lower one, decorated with a single five-pointed star, attached to the medal itself by means of a ring.

The original legislation authorized the manufacture of up to 200 medals, and the Navy Department ordered an initial lot of 175 at $1.85 each. This original amount was only sufficient to cover immediate needs: 325 (17 of which went to Marines) were ultimately awarded to Naval personnel for actions during the Civil War.

In 1942, following the abolition of the Tiffany Cross, the more familiar form of the Navy Medal with its characteristic patch of folded blue ribbon with thirteen white stars above the anchor suspension device became the norm. (US Navy)

While the Army found a serious problem keeping a steady policy as to the criteria for award of the Medal of Honor, the Navy faced an additional problem: life aboard ship was so full of danger that the practice soon arose of awarding the Medal of Honor for non-combat heroism. For example, in the period 1901–11, 48 Medals of Honor were awarded, all to Navy personnel, and all for non-combat actions. Of this number, 19 were for actions involving shipboard boiler explosions, 14 for shipboard fires, seven for life-saving, four for explosions, and four involved sinking ships. Although the heroism underlying these awards was not in question, in the view of many, the award of the Medal of Honor for actions not in the face of the enemy diluted its prestige. As a result, in 1919 the Navy instituted a "new version" of the Medal of Honor intended to be awarded for combat action only. This Medal was in the form of a cross, with an anchor on each arm of the cross, and an eagle in the center. It was designed by the Tiffany Jewelry Company of New York City, and was known accordingly as the "Tiffany Cross". The ribbon was the same design as the 1913 Medal of Honor, but featured a metal bar at the top of the ribbon inscribed "VALOUR". The Tiffany Cross proved unpopular and was discontinued in 1942, leaving the old style Medal of Honor of 1913 again available for combat related awards.

After 1919, the Medal of Honor of 1913 continued to be awarded for non-combat gallantry until 1945, when the Navy finally broke with its long-standing policy of awarding the Medal of Honor for non-combat actions. The last non-combat award of the Medal of Honor to naval personnel was made in 1945 to Boatswain's Mate 2nd Class ·Owen Hammerberg, a Navy diver whose story is told later in this book.

As with the Army, the Navy has on occasion awarded the Medal of Honor twice to the same individual. The number of those receiving the Medal of Honor for each of two separate actions involving bravery in combat is very small: four soldiers (see companion volume, Elite 95: *World War II Medal of Honor Recipients (2) Army and Air Corps*), one sailor, and two Marines. Chief Boatswain John McCloy was awarded a Medal of Honor for gallantry in China in 1900 and another for service in Mexico in 1915; Marine Gunnery Sergeant Daniel J. Daly received his for China (1900) and Haiti (1915); and Marine Major Smedley Butler for Mexico (1914) and Haiti (1915).

The Navy practice of recognizing non-combat gallantry even in peacetime created a second group of double award recipients. Until 1918, four Navy recipients had received the Medal of Honor for two separate acts of non-combat bravery, and three others had received one Medal of Honor for combat and another for non-combat actions.

Those concerned with the prestige of the Medal of Honor found it troubling that multiple awards were given to five Marines who had received an Army *and* a Navy Medal of Honor for the *same* action during

World War I. These awards reflected a lack of communication at the highest levels of the Navy and the War Departments, a situation Congress was quick to remedy. All five awards had been made in 1918 and by February 1919, Congress proscribed the practice by forbidding more than a single award to the same recipient for any reason.

Further confusion as to the identity of the award was engendered by Congress passing special legislation awarding "Congressional Medals" (sometimes even called "Medals of Honor") to famous Americans including George M. Cohan, Bob Hope, Walt Disney, and John Wayne. In at least one case, that of General Billy Mitchell, a controversial advocate of Army air power in the 1930s, it is not entirely clear even today whether Congress intended to award *the* Medal of Honor or *a* Medal of Honor.

At least three special legislation awards of the actual military Medal of Honor are recorded: Charles Lindbergh, an Army Reserve officer, received a Medal of Honor for his 1927 transatlantic flight; Commander Richard Bird, and his pilot, Machinist Mate Floyd Bennett, received the Tiffany Cross (the new Navy version intended for combat heroism only) for their flight to the North Pole in 1926. These awards caused much resentment among the ranks of Medal of Honor recipients, many of whom had received their Medals of Honor for combat action in World War I. The problem of Congressional interference has never been resolved in any satisfactory manner. In 1942, the Tiffany Cross was discontinued and the 1913 model, now mounted on a neck ribbon, was again available for both combat and non-combat gallantry.

The greater care and restraint in the award of the Medal of Honor during World War II largely restored the luster of the Medal, and the extreme heroism and self-sacrifice displayed by the recipients during this momentous period added greatly to the prestige associated with the United States' highest military award.

MEDAL OF HONOR RECIPIENTS

Commander Cassin Young, USN

The Medal of Honor entered World War II even before the declaration of war had been announced. The December 7, 1941, Sunday morning surprise attack on Pearl Harbor gave rise to 15 Medals of Honor, the first of 433 to be awarded in four years of global war.

On that morning, the USS *Vestal,* under the direction of Commander Cassin Young, was moored alongside the battleship USS *Arizona* when the Japanese attack began. Cdr Young's ship was not only strafed and bombed but was also rained with debris from the explosions aboard the mortally wounded *Arizona* close alongside.

Commander Young jumped into action by assuming command of one of the vessel's three-inch anti-aircraft guns, but when the *Arizona*'s forward magazine exploded, the explosion threw him overboard into the water, which was ablaze with burning oil. He swam back to the *Vestal* and pulled himself aboard just in time to prevent the crew from abandoning ship. The scene was chaos: several fires raged, the deck was covered with debris from the *Arizona,* and the *Vestal* had been damaged by at least two aerial bombs, one forward and one aft. Cdr Young first turned his attention to the engine room, which was filling with water from buckled plates. Only prompt shoring up of buckled bulkheads saved the *Vestal* from sinking.

Once back on the bridge, Cdr Young immediately gave orders to get his ship away from the burning *Arizona*. The engine room reported that due to ruptured steam lines, only 50lbs of the normal 250lbs of pressure was available from the boilers. The engines started. Due to the *Vestal's* damaged steering gear, she required the assistance of a tug to pull her free. However, as soon as the *Vestal* was free of the *Arizona*, she immediately developed a severe list and began to sink. Cdr Young ordered the tug to pull the vessel inshore and was successful in beaching her on a coral reef, assuring the *Vestal's* eventual salvage.

In February 1942, in a ceremony aboard the *Vestal*, Admiral Chester Nimitz presented the Medal of Honor to Cdr Young and the Navy Cross to the ship's Pharmacist Mate, Lionel Baker, for services to the vessel's wounded during the attack. Cdr Young was promoted captain in 1942 and given command of a cruiser, the USS *San Francisco*, the flagship of Rear Admiral Daniel Callaghan.

After early successes at the Battle of the Coral Sea and Midway, the United States turned to Japanese advances in the Solomon Islands. In early 1942, Japanese bomber bases on Guadalcanal in the Solomons were a threat to Australia until Marines landed and took the airfield on August 7, 1942. A long sea battle of attrition commenced: the US Navy attempted to sustain and support the Marines while the Japanese attempted to dislodge them. Neither side's task proved easy and many ships were lost. The area of sea nearby was named "Ironbound Sound" for the sunken ships littering its bottom.

On the nights of November 12–13, 1942, a strong Japanese fleet of 20 ships, including two battleships, approached Guadalcanal to attack the Marines. Admiral Callaghan had only five cruisers and eight destroyers to meet this threat. Seeing that the Japanese were disposed in two to sail *between* the two columns. A mad free-for-all resulted, with ships almost colliding with each other and occasionally firing into friendly ships in the darkness. Early on, the *San Francisco* was pounded mercilessly by

Commander Cassin Young was an experienced naval officer whose quick thinking saved the USS *Vestal* during the attack on Pearl Harbor. The *Vestal* was moored alongside the USS *Arizona* when the battleship was struck by a bomb that caused a tremendous explosion which destroyed that ship. Resisting the impulse to abandon ship, Cdr Young managed to ground his ship on a coral reef before it could sink in the deeper waters of the harbor. (US Navy)

This official US Navy photograph of the grounded USS *Vestal* shows remarkably little external damage, apart from her list, despite the fact that she had only been a few feet away from the USS *Arizona* when the battleship's magazine exploded. Not readily visible, however, was damage to the boilers and to the rudder, so severe that a tug had to be called to move the *Vestal* away from her berth. (US Navy)

two Japanese battleships and two separate hits on the *San Francisco*'s superstructure killed both Captain Young and Admiral Callaghan along with many of his staff. In addition to the badly damaged *San Francisco*, the US Navy lost eight ships, including the cruisers *Juneau* and *Atlanta*, while the Japanese lost one battleship and two destroyers. Of greatest importance, the Marine's foothold on Guadalcanal was preserved.

The *San Francisco*, despite its massive damage, was able to reach port and survived to fight again. In this action three members of her crew were awarded the Medal of Honor for saving the *San Francisco*, including Admiral Callaghan, who received the Medal of Honor posthumously for protecting the Marines on Guadalcanal. Captain Young received a posthumous award of the Navy Cross and the ship was awarded a presidential unit citation. In addition a new destroyer, the USS *Cassin Young*, was named for Captain Young. She fought with distinction throughout the remainder of the war and was retired in 1960.

Captain Henry Talmage Elrod, USMC

Immediately following the attack on Pearl Harbor, the Japanese embarked on a series of simultaneous attacks: Wake Island, Guam, Midway, Hong Kong, Luzon, and Malaya, to secure their supply lines for an advance into the Western Pacific.

By 1940, the US had realized that war with Japan could not be avoided. On Wake Island, roughly half-way between Japan and Hawaii, construction had quietly begun on an advance base for US submarines. It was defended by the 1st Marine Defense Battalion, and boasted a new airfield, but by the end of November 1941, it had not yet received any aircraft.

To remedy this situation, Marine Fighter Squadron 211 (VMF-211) was embarked on the USS *Enterprise* on November 28, 1941, and set off for Wake Island. The entire task force, under Admiral William "Bull" Halsey, set sail under "war conditions," i.e., under orders to shoot at any Japanese vessel attempting to impede their progress to the island. Along the way to Wake, every chance was taken to improve the Marine squadron's knowledge of the workings of their 12 new Grumman F4F Wildcats.

The importance the top brass attached to VMF-211's safe arrival on Wake Island was soon made clear. One aircraft, proving unserviceable, was immediately replaced. Major Paul Putnam, the squadron's Commanding Officer, was a bit bemused that:

> ... nothing should be overlooked nor any trouble spared in order to insure that I will get ashore with twelve airplanes in as near perfect condition as possible. Immediately I was given a full complement of mechs and all hands aboard continually vied with each other to see who could do the most for me. I feel a bit like the fatted calf being groomed for what ever happens to fatted calves.

Wake Island, the target of a Japanese attack in December 1941, was not deemed an important target for recapture by the American Pacific Command and, as a consequence, was bypassed. Wake became more of a practice target for new American air groups that were constantly being deployed to the theater, allowing them the opportunity to hone their skills against a moderately defended enemy target. In this 1944 photograph, an American SBD is silhouetted against the sky as it begins a run against Japanese facilities on Wake. (Official Navy Photograph)

Once ashore, VMF-211 did not have long to wait before Japanese forces arrived to test their resolve. At noon on the day after the attack on Pearl Harbor, 36 Japanese bombers arrived over Wake Island, slipping past its combat air patrol of four F4Fs in heavy cloud cover. The raiders bombed both the airfield and the camp of the civilian contractors who were building the base on Wake. During this short raid, VMF-211 lost 23 of its 55-man complement and eight Wildcats which had been parked in the open, near the landing strip. To make matters worse, upon return from the abortive combat air patrol, one of the squadron's remaining aircraft damaged its engine when the propeller struck a piece of bomb debris on landing. From this point on, the depleted squadron's ground crew was moved to spirited efforts in maintaining the four remaining serviceable squadron aircraft: these four aircraft would have to defend the airspace over the entire island against the coming onslaught.

With one stroke, the Japanese had all but destroyed VMF-211 and this attack set the pattern for all future Japanese raids on Wake. Soon the defenders of the island settled into a routine: at dawn, Marine fighters would sweep the seas looking for the submarines which directed the Japanese bombers in to the attack. The bombers themselves were to be expected from 1100 on, allowing for the 700 miles distance from the Japanese bases at Roi. When they arrived, the outnumbered aircraft of the beleaguered defenders would rise to engage them, while the Marine defenders watched from their dug-in positions.

One of these "Flying Leathernecks" was the pilot of the aircraft damaged in landing after the attack of December 8, Captain Henry T. Elrod. Born in Rebecca, Georgia, in 1905, Capt. Elrod was a veteran of 14 years peacetime service. He had enlisted in the Marine Corps in 1927 and by 1931 had obtained a commission as a second lieutenant. After eight years of ground combat experience and completion of flight training in 1935, Elrod served in various capacities in Marine aviation until he was posted to Hawaii in January 1941, where he joined VMF-211 on Oahu.

On December 10, when the Japanese bombers again appeared over Wake, the remaining four aircraft of VMF-211 were waiting for them. Captain Elrod, leading the combat air patrol, attacked 26 Japanese bombers and personally accounted for two of them. While again leading the combat air patrol on December 11, Capt. Elrod bombed and sank the IJN Destroyer *Kisargi*, the first Japanese surface vessel sunk from the air in World War II.

Following the loss of VMF-211's last planes on December 22, the squadron was converted into infantry to help defend the island against the inevitable invasion that was expected at any time. Captain Elrod, because of his prior ground combat experience, was given command of a small number of riflemen to guard the flank of the VMF-211 perimeter. When the Japanese assault finally came on December 23, 1941, VMF-211

Commander Richard Nott Antrim, shown here In a postwar picture, was executive officer of the destroyer USS *Pope*, one of the few American vessels left in the Far East when most of the Fleet returned to the eastern Pacific to regroup after Pearl Harbor. *Pope* cooperated with the British and Dutch Royal Navies in opposing the Japanese juggernaut sweeping through the Dutch East Indies, but was sunk after the disastrous Battle of the Java Sea in February 1942. (Photograph courtesy of Home of Heroes)

defended the airstrip and used a 3in. naval gun to hold off the Japanese landing barges. Capt. Elrod led the defenders in a counter-charge but was killed by a Japanese marine who lay feigning death in front of the 3in. gun position. For his actions on land and in the air, Capt. Elrod was awarded the Medal of Honor and was given a hero's burial at Arlington National Cemetery after the war.

Commander Richard Nott Antrim, USN

After Pearl Harbor, the Navy pulled most of its ships out of its remote and all too vulnerable bases in the eastern Pacific. A few ships remained, however, one of which, the destroyer USS *Pope*, cooperated with units of Allied navies to oppose and harass the Japanese advance from Singapore towards the Dutch East Indies.

The *Pope* took part in the first American naval engagements of the war – the Battle of Makassar Strait and the Battle of Badoeng Strait – and disrupted Japanese landings on Balikpapan, Borneo. During an attack on a Japanese convoy, the *Pope*'s Executive Officer, Commander Richard Antrim, so skillfully managed his ship's fire control that he was recommended for command and eventually awarded the Navy Cross for his action. Commander Antrim, born in Peru, Indiana, in 1907 was a 1931 Naval Academy graduate who had served in the surface fleet before qualifying as a dirigible pilot in 1938. Rather than being assigned as a blimp pilot, however, he was next assigned to the Asiatic Fleet as executive officer, first of the USS *Bittern*, and then, in December 1939, of the *Pope*.

As the Japanese tightened their noose around Java, the *Pope* was with an Allied fleet that was shattered at the Battle of the Java Sea on February 27–28, 1942. The *Pope* attempted to escape along with two British Royal Navy ships, heavy cruiser HMS *Exeter* and destroyer HMS *Encounter*. They were spotted by aircraft and pursued by Japanese cruisers and destroyers. Brought to bay, both Royal Navy ships were sunk. The *Pope* escaped into a rain squall but was later detected and sunk by Japanese aircraft and surface gunfire.

Virtually the entire crew reached safety either in life rafts or in the *Pope*'s only motor whaleboat. Cdr Antrim, although wounded, took charge of the survivors. Sighted by the Japanese, the survivors were taken aboard a Japanese warship, which took them to Makassar, in the southwest Celebes, where they were turned over to the Japanese Army.

Cdr Antrim and his men were taken to a prisoner of war camp at Makassar and the men soon found a very different discipline than they were used to. The Japanese believed that surrender was shameful and those guilty of this failing were men without honor. This resulted in a savage discipline where even minor infractions were punished severely. Prisoners would be beaten for any reason, or for no reason, whenever their guards deemed punishment appropriate. One such event occurred in April 1942. A Navy lieutenant did not bow low enough to one of the Japanese guards, who proceeded to beat him with a stick. Bloody and semi-conscious, the prisoner was in danger of being beaten to death, when Cdr Antrim stepped forward and tried to convince the enraged guard that his victim had intended no offense.

Soon a crowd of both guards and prisoners gathered to view this strange spectacle. The camp commandant soon convened an extremely informal hearing and decided that the nearly unconscious man should receive another 50 strokes from a thick hawser. After 15 strokes, the man lay unconscious and bloody on the ground. Cdr Antrim could stand no more; he boldly stepped forward and said that he would take the remaining punishment himself. The crowd of prisoners cheered and the Japanese commandant, apparently overcome with respect for this unexpected action, relented, sent the wounded man to the dispensary, and ordered no punishment for Cdr Antrim. After this heroic action, conditions improved somewhat, and Antrim continued to be a spokesman for the prisoners. It was for this action that Cdr Antrim was awarded the Medal of Honor.

Later, Cdr Antrim was put in charge of a labor detail responsible for making air raid protection trenches. He cleverly reworked the Japanese construction plans and obtained approval of the revised drawings. The changes Cdr Antrim introduced resulted in the trenches being constructed in the shape of a large "US", alerting Allied aircraft to the presence of American POWs in the camp. Discovery of this ruse would surely have resulted in Cdr Antrim's summary execution, but it probably saved many lives which would otherwise have been lost from mistaken Allied bombings. After the war, Cdr Antrim received the Bronze Star for this action.

Liberated at the end of the war, Cdr Antrim returned to the US and continued his naval career. On January 30, 1947, President Harry S. Truman presented the Medal of Honor and the Bronze Star to Cdr Antrim, a man who had been officially missing since the *Pope* had been sunk five years before.

Now a captain, Antrim continued his naval career with command of the destroyer USS *Turner* and the attack transport USS *Montrose*. He completed tours of staff duty in Washington, D.C., including his last assignment as Head of Amphibious Warfare Matters on the staff of the Chief of Naval Operations. He retired in 1954 with the rank of Rear Admiral to live in Mountain Home, Arkansas. He died in 1969 and is buried in Arlington National Cemetery. In remembrance of his valiant action, a Guided Missile Frigate, the USS *Richard Antrim*, was named in his honor.

Worn Allied POWs greet the liberation forces of the US Navy as they arrive at the Aomori prison camp near Yokohama in 1945. An estimated 145,000 Allied prisoners of war were held by the Japanese in WWII. The Japanese held 15,000 US prisoners of war, many captured after the fall of Bataan and Corregidor, including Medal of Honor recipients Richard O'Kane, Richard Nott Antrim, and Willibald Bianchi. The vast majority of the prisoners (108,000) were British and Empire troops, but there was also a sizeable contingent of Dutch troops taken in the battles fought throughout the Dutch possessions in the East Indies. (NARA)

Lieutenant-Commander John Duncan Bulkeley, USN

Within 12 hours of the attack on Pearl Harbor, the Japanese loosed a

massive air attack against Clark Field in the Philippines, essentially destroying American air power in the theater. An attack on the Cavite Navy Yard was expected at any time and Rear Admiral Francis Rockwell ordered his most important combat asset, Motor Torpedo Boat Squadron 3 (MTB 3), out of the immediate area. Commanded by Lieutenant-Commander John Duncan Bulkeley, MTB 3 consisted of six PT boats. This force was in essence the only Navy presence in the theater, and had been sent out to the Pacific at the end of September 1941, in answer to General MacArthur's call for reinforcements in anticipation of Japanese aggression.

John D. Bulkeley, proud descendant of several Royal Navy officers of Nelson's time, was born in New York City in 1911 and grew up in rural New Jersey. A man of great determination, when his desired appointment to the Naval Academy from the state of New Jersey was not forthcoming, he traveled to Washington at age 18 and convinced the representatives of Texas to nominate him to the Academy. Graduating from Annapolis in 1933 at the height of the Depression, Bulkeley, along with half his graduating class, was released from further military service for budgetary reasons. Not until the following year were John Bulkeley and his classmates recalled to service and commissioned as officers in the US Navy. Once commissioned, Bulkeley was assigned to the cruiser USS *Indianapolis*. As tensions with Japan grew, John Bulkeley found himself headed for Washington, D.C., on the same boat as a Japanese diplomat. Convinced that the diplomat's briefcase was full of stolen secrets, Bulkeley contrived to steal the case and swam ashore, making his way to an unimpressed Naval Intelligence Service. To avoid scandal, Bulkeley was sent as chief engineer to a gunboat, the USS *Sacramento*, on the China station. By February 1941, Bulkeley, by now a full lieutenant, was given command of Submarine Chaser Division 1, and in September of that year he was sent to the Philippines in command of MTB 3.

The PT boats of MTB 3 were of a new design: 77ft "Elco" boats, extremely heavily armed for their size with four torpedo tubes, two pairs of .50-cal. machine guns in turrets, and two fixed-mount .30-cal. machine guns. These boats were extremely fast, cruising easily at 55 knots, but the speed was attained at the expense of armor: the construction was entirely of wood, including the gun shields for the machine guns. Always present was the danger of ripping out the bottoms on coral reefs and other obstructions.

Lieutenant-Commander Bulkeley, with three boats, stood well offshore in Manila Bay when the massive Japanese air attack came just after noon on December 10. While pounding Cavite and nearby Nichols Field, his three PT boats came under air attack. By a tactic of waiting until a bomb had been released and then swerving sharply away, dive-bombing attacks were successfully thwarted. The Japanese planes then commenced strafing runs on the elusive little boats. The PTs responded with accurate

Lieutenant-Commander John Bulkeley (left) is shown in this official Navy photograph at the helm of a PT boat, similar to the ones used during the campaign in and around the Philippine Islands. Bulkeley led Motor Torpedo Boat Squadron 3, the only naval force remaining in the Philippines after Pearl Harbor. Initially consisting of six PT boats, the Squadron was in constant action against the Japanese invasion of the Philippines. After four months, which included the epic evacuation of General Douglas MacArthur and his family as well as the rescue of Philippine President Quezon from an island threatened by the Japanese advance, the Squadron lost its last two boats. (NARA)

OPPOSITE **Lieutentant-Commander Bulkeley was later transferred to the Atlantic theater. He commanded the PT boat effort during the Normandy invasion, and was then given command of the destroyer USS *Endicott* during the invasion of southern France. (US Navy)**

and effective machine gun fire, and succeeded in shooting down three Japanese aircraft.

Seeing that Cavite Navy Yard was so heavily damaged that it could no longer serve as a base for MTB 3, Bulkeley set up a makeshift base at the southern tip of the Bataan peninsula. The men lived in straw huts and scavenged for gasoline until they found an offshore barge. This was their only source of fuel, but they soon found that this gasoline had been contaminated not only with seawater, but also with a waxy substance. From then on, wax buildup in the engines was a constant worry.

After the Japanese raid on Cavite, MTB 3 became the de facto Far Eastern Fleet. Lieutenant-Commander Bulkeley returned to Cavite to ferry the wounded to the hospital, and a week later was again to rescue survivors from a refugee ship which had struck a mine. On December 22, the Japanese invaded the Philippines and two days later were on the outskirts of Manila. While the city was in flames, Lt. Cdr Bulkeley went in to scuttle Allied ships in the harbor under the noses of the occupying Japanese.

The PT boats of MTB Squadron 3 were 77ft "Elco" boats which were heavily armed with four torpedo tubes, two pairs of .50-cal. machine guns, and two .30-cal. machine guns. Here a sailor sits behind a pair of .50-cal. machine guns mounted in the broadside gun position. These boats could run at 55 knots, but this speed was at the expense of armor. The entire boat, including the gun shields on the machine guns, was constructed of plywood. (US Navy)

On January 18, 1942, a Japanese destroyer and a large troop-transport were reported off Port Binaga in Subic Bay. Two PT boats were dispatched, but only Bulkeley's boat appeared at the rendezvous point. Pressing the attack alone, one of the PT boats, 34, came under heavy fire from shore batteries but forced the attack by firing two torpedoes then retiring at high speed. There was a large explosion behind, but 34 boat's crew had other worries: one torpedo was stuck in the tube, fully armed with the propeller spinning. If the propeller was not stopped, the torpedo would explode at a preset number of revolutions. Always resourceful, one of the crew straddled the torpedo and somehow stopped the propeller by stuffing toilet paper into the chute.

Lieutenant-Commander Bulkeley's ragtag Navy, now down to four boats, continued to harass the Japanese. The next week he sank another large carrier in a close-in firefight and pursued, then personally boarded another Japanese craft. Two nights later he returned to Subic Bay to attack and sink a large Japanese ship which had been placed there as a trap.

On March 11, the four remaining boats of MTB 3 took General MacArthur, his family, and staff on a harrowing journey to Mindanao, where B-17s from Australia were waiting. Not long after, Bulkeley successfully brought Filipino President Quezon in to Mindanao from a hideout on an island 100 Japanese-controlled miles away.

On April 8, MTB 3's remaining two boats attacked a cruiser and several destroyers: their torpedoes found the cruiser, but one boat was eventually scuttled. MTB 3 was no more. Lietenant-Commander Bulkeley organized a guerrilla force in native boats to scout landing places for MacArthur's return. By April 13, the American defense was on its last legs, and Bulkeley received a direct order from General

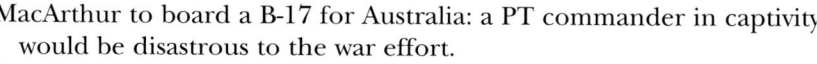

MacArthur to board a B-17 for Australia: a PT commander in captivity would be disastrous to the war effort.

Bulkeley went on to command all PT boats in the assault area during the Normandy invasion, and eventually reached the rank of Vice Admiral, retiring with 54 years of service in 1988.

Lieutenant John James "Jo Jo" Powers, USN

After the fall of the Dutch East Indies, the Japanese turned their attention to Port Moresby at the southeast corner of New Guinea, from which they could threaten Australia. The Japanese expected the US fleet to respond by going into the Coral Sea, southwest of New Guinea, where they planned to destroy it in a pincer action between two Japanese carrier-based task groups. Admiral Nimitz, US Pacific Fleet commander, was alerted to the Japanese plan by radio intercepts and reinforced Task Force 17, already in the area, with a second task force, Task Force 11, under Admiral Aubrey Fitch.

In May 1942, the aircraft carrier USS *Yorktown* was part of Task Force 17 under the command of Admiral Frank Jack Fletcher, who was to prevent the Japanese fleet from landing amphibious forces against Port Moresby in New Guinea. In aid of this invasion, the Japanese Navy had taken Guadalcanal in the Solomons chain, as well as Tulagi for a long-range reconnaissance base for their seaplanes. Admiral Fletcher decided to make a strike against this base in order to reduce the Japanese ability to detect his own carrier task force. On May 4, 1942, the *Yorktown* launched three squadrons for an attack on Tulagi, Scout Bombing Squadron 5 (VS-5), Torpedo Squadron 5 (VT-5), and Bombing Squadron 5 (VB-5). Flying with VB-5 was Lieutenant John James Powers, who would make a name for himself that day.

John James Powers was born in New York City in 1912 and graduated from the Naval Academy in 1935. After five years with the surface fleet, he completed flight training in 1940 and was assigned to VB-5, which had been equipped with SBD-3 "Dauntless" dive-bombers assigned to the *Yorktown*.

Arriving over Tulagi at approximately 0800 on May 4, 1942, the attack group found a Japanese invasion force at anchor in the harbor. The men of VB-5 pushed their dive-bombers into steep 70-degree angle dives from 10,000ft and dropped their 1,000lb bombs on the Japanese fleet. Unfortunately, due to differences in air temperature between 10,000ft and the bomb release point, the telescopic bombsights of the SBD-3s became hopelessly fogged, making aim uncertain at best. Out of 15 individual attacks, none resulted in damage to their targets. On a second strike mission later that day, Lt. Powers was to have better luck. VB-5 found three Japanese mine sweepers near Savo Island, northeast of Tulagi. This time Lt. Powers' aim was truer in the attack; he was able to hit and sink one of the Japanese vessels with a 1,000lb bomb.

On May 7, 1941, the rival battle fleets neared each other in the Coral Sea. At 0735, scout planes from the *Yorktown* located the Japanese task force, which included the light carrier IJN *Shoho*, north of the Louisa Archipelago. Admiral Fletcher immediately ordered a strike against the Japanese task force. At 0944, SBD-3 dive-bombers of VS-5 launched

Lieutenant John James Powers is pictured wearing his winter service dress blue uniform.

On May 8, 1942, the Naval forces of Japan and America met in the first sea battle in history where the members of the surface fleets in action never saw the opposing fleet. Coral Sea was to be the first of many carrier battles during the Pacific war. In this official Navy photograph, the IJN *Shokaku* circles frantically to avoid the bombs falling around her. This photograph clearly shows the effects of that bombing as a fire rages on the forecastle. (US Navy)

from the *Yorktown* and proceeded to their intended target. Arriving at the battle scene at 1100, VB-5 closed in to attack the *Shoho*, previously damaged by a raid from the USS *Lexington*. Unaffected by the lens fogging that had so plagued the Tulagi raid, Lt. Powers pressed a successful attack that caused a tremendous explosion aboard the *Shoho*, engulfing her in flames.

Following the attack on the *Shoho*, Lt. Powers, as Squadron Gunnery Officer, urged the latest possible bomb release to achieve maximum accuracy in the dive-bomb attack. "I am going to get a hit if I have to lay it on their flight deck," he declared.

May 8 dawned on the second day of the Battle of the Coral Sea with the advantage clearly in the favor of the US Navy; the Americans lost one destroyer and a fleet oiler while the Japanese lost their first aircraft carrier of the war. VB-5 launched against the main Japanese strike force and caught up with them at approximately 1100. The target selected was the aircraft carrier IJN *Shokaku*, previously attacked unsuccessfully by VS-5. VB-5 was resolved that they would be more successful.

When his turn came, Lt. Powers pushed his aircraft over from 10,000ft into a steep dive. Although hit by 20mm fire from an attacking Zero that wounded both Lt. Powers and his gunner, he pressed his attack in spite of the flames which enveloped his plane. Pulling out at an extremely low altitude, Lt. Powers released a 1,000lb bomb that struck the *Shokaku*'s flight deck, causing extensive damage. Lt. Powers did not survive his daring attack, however. Too low to pull his damaged aircraft out of its dive, he crashed into the sea near the Japanese flattop he had just hit.

The Battle of the Coral Sea must be considered a draw in view of the losses suffered by both sides (the US lost the aircraft carrier *Lexington* while the Japanese lost the carrier *Shoho* with the *Shokaku* heavily damaged) but the Japanese threat to Australia had been averted, never to be renewed.

Sergeant Clyde Thomason, USMCR

In summer 1942, the US Navy decided upon a diversionary action to distract Japanese attention while planning a move on Guadalcanal. Makin Island, in the Gilbert chain, was chosen. The Japanese had neutralized Makin and nearby Tarawa within two days of the Pearl Harbor attack, but had not occupied them in any strength. The job was given to Lieutenant-Colonel Evans Carlson, commanding officer of the newly formed Second Marine Raider Battalion, better known as Carlson's Raiders. Carlson and his second in command, Major James Roosevelt, son of the President, would personally lead a small force of Raiders to attack the Japanese garrison and withdraw before the Japanese could respond in force.

Clyde Thomason, a sergeant in the 2nd Marine Raider Battalion, was chosen to play a key role in the raid. A native of Atlanta, Georgia, Thomason enlisted in the Marine Corps at the age of 20 in 1934 and served in China. In 1939, he was mustered out, only to rejoin the Corps Reserves after Pearl Harbor. Volunteering for the Raiders, Sgt. Thomason's 6'4" frame almost kept him out of the commando-style unit, but he persevered and was assigned to the 2nd Battalion in the Pacific in April, 1942. During preparations for the Makin raid, Sgt. Thomason was put in charge of the advance element.

Early on the morning of August 17, 1942, two companies of the 2nd Raider Battalion, comprising approximately 200 Marines, were delivered close ashore by the submarines *Argonaut* and *Nautilus*, embarking in rubber boats for the final trip to the shore. Things did not go as planned. Difficulties began almost immediately; none of the motors on the rubber boats would start, causing delay and confusion. Finally ashore, one of the Marines accidentally discharged a weapon, putting to rest any hope of secrecy. The alerted Japanese soon counterattacked the Raiders as they were still deploying ashore. A confused firefight ensued, with Japanese snipers and machine gunners adding to the terror of repeated Banzai charges. Sgt. Thomason forced his way into a building which concealed a sniper and killed him before he could resist. Thomason, however, was primarily concerned with directing his platoon's fire, and died leading his men to the attack in the predawn confusion.

Although unaware of it, the Marines had not only outnumbered the Japanese defenders, but after dealing with two Banzai charges, they had virtually wiped out the Japanese garrison. Late in the morning, two Japanese aircraft bombed the island, but the Marines suffered no casualties. Two hours later, two Japanese seaplanes landed in the lagoon, but they were quickly destroyed by the Raiders. This provoked a response from the ten Japanese fighter aircraft which had accompanied the seaplanes. These aircraft bombed and strafed the Marines for an hour, but caused few casualties. Another air raid followed later in the afternoon.

Fearing Japanese reinforcements, Lieutenant-Colonel Carlson decided to withdraw early in the evening. Unfortunately, the motors on the rubber boats were still inoperative and only 80 men managed to paddle through the surf and Carlson and most of his remaining 120 men were low on ammunition by this time, and after a Japanese patrol attacked the perimeter during the night, Col. Carlson decided to send a message of surrender to the Japanese. Luckily, the message did not get

Sergeant Clyde Thomason is shown on leave some time before the raid on Makin Island in August 1942. Sgt. Thomason, a veteran of prewar China service, re-enlisted after the attack on Pearl Harbor, and was assigned to Carlson's Raiders in April 1942. Tall and imposing, Sgt. Thomason was put in charge of an advance element in the attack on Makin Island. (USMC)

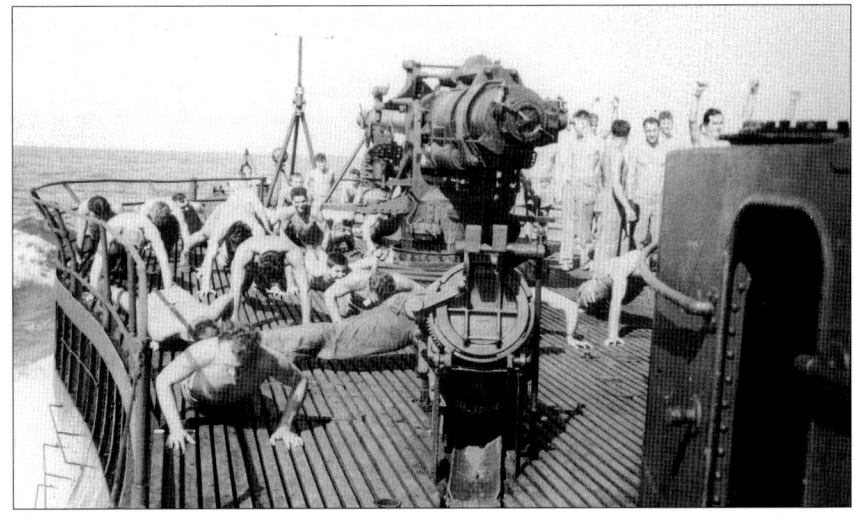

USS *Nautilus* and her sister USS *Argonaut* were "Cruiser" submarines, an unsuccessful Navy experiment of building large submarines with extended range. In reality, both vessels proved to be unhandy underwater and were relegated to activities that would render them less vulnerable to attack, such as delivering this group of Carlson's Raiders to the Makin Island raid. (US Navy)

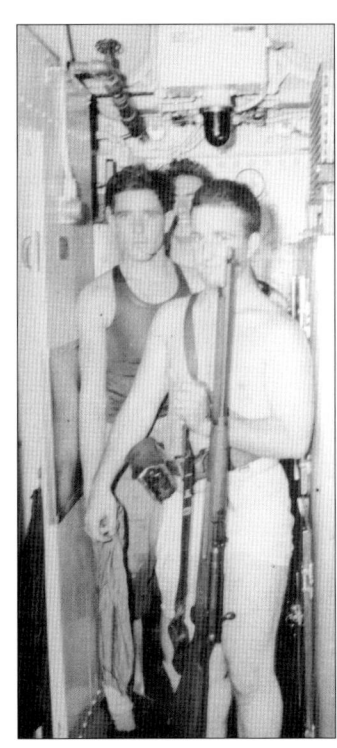

Two Marine Raiders aboard the *Nautilus* show off some Japanese souvenirs on their way back from the Makin raid. After the raid, Makin and nearby Tarawa were reinforced by the Japanese, which caused the Marines great difficulties during the attack on Tarawa in November 1943. (US Navy)

through. At this time, Carlson permitted those who wished to make another attempt to reach the submarines to try, and another 50 raiders managed to get through the surf.

At dawn the Marines found themselves not only in control, but practically the only men alive on the Island. Patrols reported no resistance and counted 83 Japanese dead. Carlson and his men were subjected to four more air raids that day, but suffered no further losses. By midnight of August 18, the remaining force re-embarked on the submarines and proceeded to Pearl Harbor. In the confusion, nine Raiders were left behind on Makin along with the 19 dead. These men evaded capture until August 30, when they surrendered to the Japanese and were taken to Kwajalein Island, where they were beheaded.

In 1999, a mass grave containing the remains of 19 Marines and one Islander was discovered on Makin Island. The bodies were identified using forensic techniques and returned to the United States for reburial. While six were buried in their hometowns, the remaining 13 were buried at Arlington National Cemetery, all with full military honors. Sergeant Clyde Thomason, one of the 13, finally returned home from the Makin raid after 59 years.

Signalman 1st Class Douglas Albert Munro, USCG

In July 1942, the US learned of Japanese troop concentrations and a new air base being built on Guadalcanal. This Japanese presence on Guadalcanal threatened the Allied strategic offensive against Japanese-held Rabaul.

A former Australian base at the eastern end of New Britain, Rabaul was the Gibraltar of the southwest Pacific. With its two harbors, it dominated New Guinea and threatened Allied communication and supply lines with Australia. Rabaul was much more than a naval base, however, it was also the hub of the Japanese air base system in the southwest Pacific, home to over 300 aircraft. Further, 800 miles away on Truk, two carrier air groups equipped with another 300 aircraft stood by to reinforce Rabaul, should the need arise.

Recognizing that Rabaul could not be taken by direct assault, the US used aerial bombardment. In view of the fact that the Allies had very few

When President Franklin D. Roosevelt authorized Coast Guard personnel to man Navy transport ships, 23-year-old Signalman 1st Class Douglas Munro transferred to the transport *Hunter Liggett*. The 535ft ship could transport 700 men and deliver them to an enemy shore along with two large landing craft and 35 smaller "Higgins" boats. Munro became an expert at operating the 36ft long, wooden "Higgins" boat in landing troops under fire. (US Coast Guard)

aircraft in the theater with the range to bomb Rabaul and return to base, an island-hopping plan had been decided upon. US forces would move up the Solomon chain from Guadalcanal in the southeast, through New Georgia, to Bougainville in the northwest, all the while establishing air bases from which to attack Rabaul. The Japanese fortification of Guadalcanal directly threatened this strategy, and had to be dealt with immediately.

On August 7, 1942, the First Marine Division under Major General Alexander Vandegrift launched the first major amphibious offensive in the Pacific war, simultaneously attacking Guadalcanal and nearby Tulagi Island.

Coast Guardsmen operated the landing craft to put the Marines ashore. For the first time, the Coast Guard, due to its extensive experience with the handling of small boats, was given the important task of augmenting the Navy in transporting the Marines to the invasion beaches. Among them, Signalman 1st Class Douglas Munro became the only Coast Guardsman ever to receive the Medal of Honor, and he remains to date the only person whose memory is commemorated by a statue inside Coast Guard Headquarters.

Douglas Munro was born in 1919 in Vancouver, British Columbia, where his parents were temporarily residing. Returning to Washington state, young Douglas grew up in Cle Elum, graduating from high school in 1937. In 1939, as the threat of war loomed, he chose to enlist in the US Coast Guard because of its primarily life-saving mission. Until mid-1941 he served aboard the USCG cutter *Spencer*, where he won a rating as a signalman.

In June 1941, even before the US formally entered the war, President Franklin D. Roosevelt ordered the Coast Guard to provide guardsmen to serve along with Navy personnel aboard Navy vessels as well as operate large transports. Munro voluntarily transferred to one of these, the *Hunter Liggett*, one of the largest transports in the Pacific. The *Hunter Liggett* was a 535ft, 13,712-ton ship that could transport almost 700 men, 35 landing craft (the "Higgins" boat) and two larger landing craft which could carry tanks in addition to men. Munro was to become expert in the handling of the "Higgins" boats.

The "Higgins" boats were 36ft long and made entirely of wood without any armor protection. These boats had blunt-nosed plywood hulls, making them both slow and vulnerable even to small arms fire. They were lightly armed with only a pair of .30-cal. machine guns.

The *Hunter Liggett* sailed from New Zealand to join the Guadalcanal task force gathered at sea at the end of July, and on August 7 the twin assaults on Guadalcanal and Tulagi began. Signalman Munro delivered his cargo of Marines onto the beach under heavy fire. Tulagi was secured the following day, August 8. Unfortunately, there would be a different story on Guadalcanal.

General Vandegrift's main force landed without opposition on Guadalcanal and moved inland, but for some reason the supplies that landed along with the troops were left to pile up in disorder on the beach. Soon there was so much chaos on the beach that many recently landed troops found themselves wandering around in confusion. By afternoon, the move inland had slowed, and by dark, defense lines were set up.

The airfield was taken by late afternoon of the second day as the Japanese defenders retreated in disarray. Japanese indecisiveness came to an end that night, however, when a Japanese cruiser force broke up the US naval screen in the Battle of Savo Island. The US support ships, left undefended, sailed away, still partially loaded with troops and supplies. They left behind 17,000 Marines on Guadalcanal and Tulagi. The Marines remained unreinforced until the arrival of dive-bombers and fighters on August 20.

Meanwhile, the Japanese decided to retake Guadalcanal. Lieutenant-General Harayukichi Hyakutake was given 50,000 men to do the job. First, he began immediate heavy bombing day and night, and then he landed 1,000 troops under Colonel Kiyono Ichiki (known as the Ichiki Detachment) east of Henderson Field and attempted an assault on Marine positions on the Ilu river. Most of the Ichiki Detachment was destroyed in one determined Banzai attack, in spite of Marine defenses that were stretched to the limit.

Thus began the grim struggle for Guadalcanal, with each side committing more and more troops and matériel to the campaign. By mid-October the Japanese managed to land 20,000 troops, greatly outnumbering Vandegrift, until the Marines, too, were reinforced, bringing their numbers up to 23,000.

With Allied aircraft operating from Henderson Field, Japanese naval dominance was once again disputed. During the six months of the campaign, a large number of naval actions were fought. So many ships on both sides were sunk that the strait between Guadalcanal and Florida Island became known as "Iron Bottom Sound". The Coast Guard had returned with the Navy, and both were fully occupied.

On September 20, Signalman Munro attempted a small boat rescue off the coast of Savo Island for the crew of a downed Navy dive-bomber. The mission was boldly handled with Signalman Munro bringing his boat within 300yds of the shore under enemy fire, only to find the flyers had already been rescued.

While the US and Japanese navies fought a savage war of attrition, the Marines on Guadalcanal were in position to go deeper into the island's interior jungle, west across the Matanikau River. On September 27, after several unsuccessful attempts to cross the river, Marine Lieutenant-Colonel Lewis B. "Chesty" Puller embarked three companies of his Seventh Marines in landing craft and attempted an end run by

Close cooperation between the naval and ground forces was one tactic that was to come out of the war in the Pacific. Here Marines on the Island of Guam express gratitude to the Coast Guard sailors that operated many of the landing craft that brought them safely to the beachheads of the Pacific war. Even more appreciated was the rescue function of the Coast Guard "Higgins" boats that often waited after landing troops to pick up casualties. (NARA)

landing 500 men on the far side of the river. Munro was in charge of the landing craft transporting Puller's men from Lunga Point to a small cove west of Point Cruz.

Supported by naval gunfire from the destroyer USS *Monssen*, the landing appeared to be unopposed. This situation was not to last. When the Marines reached a ridge several hundred yards from the beach, a large Japanese force appeared and pushed them back. By this time, Munro had returned to his base at Lunga Point. The Marines had no way to communicate with Signalman Munro to request assistance, so they resorted to scratching the word "HELP" in the sand. Some sources say that the word was spelled out in underwear. Whatever the medium, the message was spotted by a Navy patrol plane passing over a ridge not far from the beach. While the *Monssen* directed covering fire for Col. Puller's men, the same landing craft that had delivered the Marines were now called upon to extricate them. Signalman Munro led his Coast Guardsmen back to Point Cruz.

The situation facing the Marines and the rescuers was grim. The Japanese were dug in on the ridge, a position the Marines had recently vacated. An overlapping field of fire was assured by another position to the east of the landing area.

As Munro boldly led five of his wooden "Higgins" boats inshore, casualties among the boat crews rapidly mounted. While the Marines re-embarked, the Japanese rushed the beach. Munro interposed his frail craft between the Japanese and the boats carrying off the Marines. The entire 500-man Marine landing force escaped, but before the maneuver had been completed, Signalman Munro was killed by enemy fire. His crew, with two members wounded, successfully completed the evacuation. Without Munro's selfless sacrifice, many Marines of the Seventh Regiment would undoubtedly have died that day.

A month after Munro's death, his parents received notification from the Navy Department that their son had been awarded the Medal of Honor, which was formally presented to them by President Roosevelt in a ceremony at the White House in May 1943.

Signalman 1st Class Douglas Munro was buried on September 28, 1942, on Guadalcanal, but his remains were brought home after the war and interred in his hometown of Cle Elum, Washington. His achievements are remembered not only in the hearts of all members of the Coast Guard, but also in a Coast Guard cutter named in his honor.

Sergeant John Basilone, USMC

In mid-September 1942, Marine Sergeant John Basilone found himself heading for the South Pacific with the objective of reinforcing the beleaguered American troops on Guadalcanal. Sgt. Basilone, a member of 7th Marine Regiment, 1st Marine Division, Company "C", was not a raw recruit as were most of his men. Born in Buffalo, New York, in 1916, he had enlisted in the US Army when he reached the age of 18. Three years service in the Philippines earned him the nickname, "Manila John". Discharged in 1937, Basilone returned to the United States, where he worked as a truck driver prior to re-enlisting, this time in the Marine Corps in 1940.

By October 1942, the situation for the Marines on the 'Canal had become quite grim; US forces were dwindling while Japanese numbers were steadily growing. By mid-October, the Japanese forces under Lieutenant-General Harukichi Hyakutake reached 20,000 men, when Hiyakutake deemed it the right time to begin an all out effort to retake the island. As part of this offensive, the Japanese 2nd Division attacked American positions along the Matanijau River west of Henderson Field.

The 7th Marines were stationed along a defensive line some 2,500yds long, extending to the bank of the Lunga River, north of Henderson Field. Sgt. Basilone commanded two sections of water-cooled .30-cal. machine guns in a defensive position in the Lunga area, just north of Henderson Field. On the night of October 24, the Japanese began their attack by hitting Sgt. Basilone's position with mortar fire in order to soften it up prior to an infantry assault. As the Japanese infantry pushed forward, they hammered Sgt. Basilone's position with grenades and mortar fire, leaving one of his sections with only two able-bodied men.

Forced to make do with the material at hand, Sgt. Basilone was virtually a one-man army, constantly shifting his position to keep the Japanese off balance and guessing at the true strength of the American opposition that they faced. Under heavy enemy fire, Sgt. Basilone moved an extra gun into position and manned it, then personally repaired a second gun and fired it until replacements arrived. Later, with ammunition in critically low supply, Sgt. Basilone cut his way through enemy lines in order to bring ammunition to his beleaguered gunners. During this attack, an eyewitness observed that, "Basilone had a machine gun on the go for three days and nights without sleep, rest, or food … He was in a good emplacement, and causing the Japs lots of trouble, not only firing his machine gun but also using his pistol."

By the end of the third night's action, Sgt. Basilone had held the line and saved his men from being overrun in the face of determined Japanese attacks; some 38 enemy bodies were lying in a mound before the muzzle of Sgt. Basilone's machine gun.

The Japanese attacking forces lost over 3,500 men in the effort to take Henderson Field. The heroic actions of the American forces on the perimeter defense of the airfield blunted the Japanese efforts to retake Guadalcanal. Following these actions, the Japanese were forced to begin a withdrawal to the eastern end of the island. During this time Army replacements supplemented, and eventually replaced, the beleaguered Marines. Organized resistance to American forces did not end until February 1943, finishing a bloody six-month campaign. Finally, on February 9, 1943, the island was declared secure. The campaign had cost the Japanese 25,000 lives while the US lost more than 1,000 Marines and almost 500 Army personnel.

After being awarded the Medal of Honor, Sgt. Basilone returned to the United States in order to help raise money in the Third War Loan

Sergeant "Manila" John Basilone, a Marine who had prewar service with the US Army in the Philippines (hence the nickname) was the only US Marine to receive both the Navy Cross and the Congressional Medal of Honor during World War II. (USMC)

The Battle for Guadalcanal would hinge on supply and ultimately it was the Japanese inability to keep their forces up to strength that was to play a decisive role in their loss of the island. Here Marine, Navy, and Coast Guard personnel work together to off-load supplies from "Higgins" boats. In the background is the wrecked *Kinugawa Maru*, sunk and run aground on November 15, 1942, as she attempted to deliver troops to the northern part of the island. (Official Navy Photograph)

Drive. He was successful in raising $1,300,000 for the war effort, yet "Manila" John was not happy in this new role. He felt that the war was passing him by, leaving him feeling like a "museum piece" selling war bonds while his buddies were fighting desperate battles in the Pacific.

"I'm a plain soldier, and I want to stay one" he told authorities. True to his word, he volunteered for the 1945 invasion of Iwo Jima, where he was killed in a brave attack on an enemy bunker. This final action earned him a posthumous Navy Cross and made him the only Marine to receive both the Navy Cross and the Medal of Honor during World War II.

First Lieutenant Jefferson Joseph DeBlanc, USMC

When VMF-112 arrived at Guadalcanal in November 1942, the battle for CACTUS, the Allied code name for Guadalcanal, was far from over. For more than three months the battle for the island had been waged by land, sea, and air, with mixed results. VMF-112 of the 11th Marine Air Group had been sent to the South Pacific to replace one of the battle-reduced squadrons that had been stationed on Guadalcanal since the battle began.

VMF-112, under the command of Major Paul Fontana, was a unit lacking combat experience. Most of its members were sent to Guadalcanal with only four hours in the aircraft type in which they would be fighting, the F4F Wildcat. The squadron received its baptism of fire on

November 11, 1942, flying an interceptor mission against Japanese aircraft attacking the supply fleet off Guadalcanal. In the next two months, one of its junior members, First Lieutenant Jefferson J. DeBlanc flew a variety of missions in which he downed three enemy aircraft.

By January 1943, Guadalcanal was generally secure from Japanese attack and was being used as a base to launch offensive raids against enemy targets on nearby island groups. During one such mission near New Georgia Island, Lt. DeBlanc would fight a gallant action that brought him the Medal of Honor.

Jefferson Joseph DeBlanc, a native of Louisiana, was born in Lockport on February 15, 1921. In June 1940, as a student at Southwestern Louisiana Institute, he signed up for the Civilian Pilot Program with the goal of becoming a military pilot. In 1942, after the completion of his flight training, DeBlanc was commissioned 2nd Lieutenant in the US Marine Corps. Following an advanced course at a Carrier Training Unit in San Diego, Lt. DeBlanc was assigned to VMF-112 and promptly found himself on his way to war in the South Pacific.

Lt. DeBlanc's mission on January 31, 1943, was to lead a flight of six Wildcats as escorts for 12 dive-bombers and torpedo planes on a raid against Japanese shipping near Kolombangara Island. The 250-mile trip to the island only allowed the Wildcats a bare 15 minutes of combat before having to begin the return trip to Guadalcanal.

The mission was dogged by problems from the beginning. First, the dive-bombers were late for the rendezvous, and it was after 1500 when the Wildcats formed up and climbed to altitude. Then one of the fighters reported a rough engine a short time into the flight, so he aborted and returned to base. Not long after this pilot's departure, a second pilot reported difficulties with his fuel gauges and left the mission. A bare 30 minutes into the flight, Lt. DeBlanc was already down to six fighters! As Lt. DeBlanc was later to learn, his own aircraft was far from being in perfect fighting condition; for some reason fuel consumption was abnormally high, leaving him with very limited fuel reserves for the coming action.

Leading his section to Kolombangara at an altitude of 14,000ft, Lt. DeBlanc noticed that the enemy airfield where he expected to meet opposition was empty. As the SBDs made their attack runs on the Japanese ships, flak began to burst among the American formations and two of the Wildcats peeled off to strafe the Japanese ships. The accuracy of the dive-bombers was off, no hits were scored on enemy ships. As the bombers pulled out of their attack dives, they were in turn attacked by two Japanese Mitsubishi "Pete" float planes, antiquated biplanes, yet still capable of dealing with unprotected American dive-bombers. Lt. DeBlanc, who was flying "top cover", picked up urgent calls from the dive-bombers that they were under attack. Diving to 1,000 feet, Lt. DeBlanc and his wingman engaged the Japanese planes. Lt. DeBlanc's

In an official Marine Corps photograph, Captain Jefferson DeBlanc is pictured in his winter dark green wool service dress. As a Marine Corp aviator, Capt. DeBlanc was entitled to wear the golden wings of a Naval aviator. (USMC photograph)

marksmanship made short work of both Japanese aircraft, allowing the American bombers to reconstruct their defensive formation for the trip back to Guadalcanal.

At this point, a radio call from a VMF-112 pilot alerted Lt. DeBlanc that the long-expected Japanese Zeros were on their way. Climbing to attack, Lt. DeBlanc remained undetected by the Japanese, who were intent on the other VMF-112 Wildcats. Lt. DeBlanc bagged his first Zero as it flew right into his sights, unaware of his presence. As the Wildcats engaged the Zeros, a wild aerial mêlée ensued with both sides losing aircraft and becoming entangled with each other. Lt. DeBlanc and his wingman began to fly in a scissoring defensive formation in order to keep each others' tails clear of Zeros. During one such pass, Lt.DeBlanc's wingman was hit by a Zero, but fire from Lt. DeBlanc's guns forced the Zero to pull away.

Soon Lt. DeBlanc found himself alone, his sole companion having been shot down and the rest of the section scattered in the mêlée with the Zeros. Low on fuel and with the mission completed, Lt. DeBlanc could have headed for Guadalcanal with good conscience, until he noticed enemy aircraft were re-forming for a run at the retreating dive-bombers. Hoping to lure the Japanese away, Lt. DeBlanc engaged the enemy fighters by making a head-on attack on one of the Zeros. The six .50-cals. of DeBlanc's Wildcat caused the Zero to catch fire as the planes rushed at each other. Worried that the Zero might crash into him, Lt. DeBlanc held down his trigger and the Japanese aircraft exploded. There was no time for self-congratulation, however, as the first Japanese plane's wingman began attacking. In this engagement, Lt. DeBlanc shot down the second Zero, but sustained severe damage from the guns of the remaining Japanese planes.

After bailing out Lt. DeBlanc played dead in his parachute harness as the Japanese fighter that had shot him down circled. He had been taught in survival training that in a water landing, it was best to release the harness prior to hitting the water. Lt. DeBlanc, however, misjudged his altitude and released his harness too soon, plunging 40 feet into the

Pictured is a Marine Corps Grumman F4F at Henderson Field, similar to the one flown by Capt. DeBlanc on his escort mission. The Grumman Corporation was known as the "Iron Works" by Navy and Marine aviators because of the durability of their product and the tremendous punishment they could take and still bring their pilots home. (US Navy)

water. Lt. DeBlanc spent the next six hours swimming back to Kolombangara Island. Once on the island, Lt. DeBlanc hid in an abandoned hut, but was picked up by a native tribe that soon traded him to another tribe for a bag of rice. Eventually, an Australian coast watcher found Lt. DeBlanc and radioed for assistance. A PBY was dispatched to pick up Lt. DeBlanc and return him to Guadalcanal to rejoin VMF-112.

Lt. DeBlanc was promoted captain and six months later returned to the United States, where he was presented with the Medal of Honor. He later returned to combat flying with VMF-212 during the Okinawa campaign, where he shot down his last Japanese aircraft, bringing his final tally to nine. After the war Capt. DeBlanc entered the Marine Corps Reserve, rising to the rank of colonel, and took a career in teaching. As of early 2002, Jefferson DeBlanc was enjoying retirement in Louisiana.

Captain John Philip Cromwell, USN

On November 5, 1943, Captain John Cromwell was summoned to the office of the Commander Submarines, Pacific, Admiral Charles Lockwood, for a briefing on a new operation that was about to take place in the Central Pacific, code-named GALVANIC, the invasion of Tarawa. Capt. Cromwell was to ship aboard the USS *Sculpin* to a position off the island of Truk. Once on station, the *Sculpin* was to be joined by three other American submarines: USS *Searaven*, *Spearfish*, and *Apogon*. Together they would act as a wolf pack under Capt. Cromwell's command. His orders were to interdict any Japanese surface units that might attempt to reach the landing site at Tarawa from their bases at Truk.

Capt. Cromwell was a highly placed officer who, by late 1943, had extensive experience with the tactical and technical difficulties that plagued the US submarine service. Born in 1901, he had graduated from the Naval Academy in 1924, and spent the customary two years with the surface fleet before transferring to the "Silent Service". When war broke out in 1941, he was in command of Submarine Divisions 43 and 44. In addition to the knowledge of the GALVANIC invasion, he had also been made aware that the Japanese naval code had been cracked by Navy code breakers, who had been providing highly accurate information about Japanese shipping. At the end of the meeting, Admiral Lockwood cautioned Capt. Cromwell to make sure that this information did not fall into the hands of the enemy in case of capture.

On the way to the rendezvous point, the *Sculpin* made a radar contact on a Japanese convoy. The captain of the boat, Commander Fred Connaway, ordered an attack approach on the Japanese vessels. During this approach, a Japanese lookout spotted the *Sculpin*'s periscope and a destroyer, the *Yamagumo*, moved to investigate. Cdr Connaway broke off the attack and ordered the *Sculpin* to dive deep to avoid the destroyer. Later in the night, Cdr Connaway surfaced to make a high-speed "end run" to catch up with the convoy. Unfortunately, as the *Sculpin* surfaced, she found herself within 6,000yds of the *Yamagumo*, which had been left

Captain John Cromwell was one of a select group of officers who had knowledge of both the forthcoming American invasion of Tarawa as well as the American code-breaking activities against the Japanese, code-named MAGIC. When the USS *Sculpin* was heavily damaged by the Japanese, he voluntarily rode her to the bottom of the sea rather than run the risk of being captured by the Japanese. (US Navy)

This rare photograph shows a beautiful bow on view of the USS *Sculpin*, highlighting the clean lines of the American fleet boats. (US Navy)

behind by the convoy commander to deal with the American submarine. Cdr Connaway immediately ordered the *Sculpin* to crash dive as the Japanese destroyer began its depth charge run. During this attack the *Sculpin*'s depth gauge was damaged.

After the apparent end of the depth charge attack, Cdr Connaway felt safe enough to give the order to bring the sub up to periscope depth, but due to the damaged depth gauge, the *Sculpin* unexpectedly broke the surface near the Japanese destroyer. Frantically, Cdr Connaway attempted to dive the boat, but the *Sculpin* was in poor shape and the *Yamagumo*'s gunfire caused severe damage to the sub's pressure hull. Realizing that the *Sculpin*'s only chance lay in speed, Cdr Connaway ordered "Action Surface" in a vain attempt to escape the destroyer. As all hands went to battle stations, a round from the *Yamagumo* struck the bridge and killed Cdr Connaway and the bridge crew, as well as the executive officer in the conning tower. Lieutenant G. E. Brown, the engineering officer, suddenly in command of the sub, ordered the *Sculpin* abandoned.

Capt. Cromwell told Lt. Brown, "I can't go with you. I know too much." He remained alone aboard the *Sculpin* as she made her final plunge to the bottom. For his heroic action, Capt. Cromwell became the highest-ranking officer of the submarine service to receive the Medal of Honor during World War II.

Colonel David Monroe Shoup, USMC

After victory at Guadalcanal in the Solomons, attention shifted to the Gilbert Islands, which had to be taken prior to a strike against a more important target, the Marshall Islands, whose airfields and fleet anchorages were considered crucial to the systematic march across the Pacific. Betio, the chief island of the Tarawa Atoll, contained an airfield of strategic importance in the future campaign against the Marshalls. An assault force of 35,000 men was assembled under the 5th Amphibious Corps, consisting of soldiers of the 27th Army Infantry Division and Marines of the 2nd Marine Division, under the command of Major General Julian Smith. The plan called for simultaneous attacks on Makin Island and Betio Island. Accordingly, the assault troops were divided into a Northern and a Southern Attack Force. The Northern Force's mission was to take Makin Island. This force was led by Rear Admiral Kelly Turner, 5th Amphibious Corps commander, and consisted of the men of the 27th Infantry Division. The Southern Attack Force, heading for the main objective of Betio Island, was made up of elements of the 2nd, 6th, and 8th Marines, veterans of the Solomons campaign, in addition to the 10th and 18th Marines, comprising in all some 5,000 men.

Makin Island, with a Japanese garrison of no more than 800 men, took the 27th Division three days to capture, but the Army's losses were light. The assault on Betio, however, was the bloodiest battle in Marine Corps history to that date, and under the title of "Tarawa", retains even today a hallowed place in the history of the Corps.

Tarawa, part of the British mandate in the Gilbert Islands before the war, was subdued by the Japanese on December 10, 1941. Following the Makin Island raid in August 1942, the Japanese occupied and began to construct elaborate defenses on Tarawa. The natural caves were incorporated into a defense line anchored with camouflaged concrete bombproofs, all interconnected by communication trenches. Rear Admiral Keiji Shibasaki had 5,000 tough Japanese Marines of the Seventh Special Naval Landing Force well supplied with automatic weapons, supported by four eight-inch Naval guns and 14 tanks. This formidable force had no other job than to protect an island 1 $^3/_4$ miles long and $^1/_4$-mile wide. Admiral Shibasaki pronounced himself confident that one million men could not take his island in one hundred years.

The science of amphibious assaults in the Pacific was in an embryonic state, both with regard to planning and equipment. At Tarawa, treacherous tides over a coral reef barrier were ignored by planners, who relied upon a World War I style grand barrage from naval vessels and aircraft to subdue the formidable Japanese defenses.

The landing at Betio on November 20, 1943, did not go well. The tides were insufficient to carry the "Higgins" boats over the coral reef barrier, leaving the troops to wade ashore 500yds. The remaining troops, carried in amphibious tracked vehicles called "Alligators", fared no better; 90 of a total of 125 "Alligators" sank before reaching the beach. The Japanese held fire until the first wave of "Alligators" hit the beach, then they opened up a murderous fire on the remaining waves as they approached the beach. In all, 1,500 of 5,000 Marines sent ashore that day became casualties.

Once a beachhead was established, the first Japanese counterstrike wiped out effective US communication with the fleet, making fire control difficult. Colonel David Monroe Shoup, Divisional Operations Officer, was in command of the Marines ashore. By the time of Tarawa, Col. Shoup had already had a very full 17-year career in the Marines. A native of Indiana and a 1926 De Pauw University ROTC graduate, he began his military career with the Army, but after a month, 2nd Lieutenant Shoup accepted a commission in the Marines. He then spent two years getting through the Marine Officer's Basic School in Philadelphia because he was sent off for temporary duty three times, the last time to Tiensin, China, for a year. From 1929 to 1931, Lt. Shoup was assigned to the Marine contingent aboard the battleship USS *Maryland*, the same ship that would be the flagship for the invasion of Tarawa a dozen years later. In 1934, 1st Lt. Shoup returned to China for two years, and then served as an instructor at Quantico, Virginia. In 1940, Capt. Shoup joined the

Colonel David Shoup was in command of the 5,000 Marines ashore in the November 1943 invasion of Tarawa, one of the bloodiest battles in the Pacific war. Despite an infected leg wound, Col. Shoup, out of radio contact with the invasion fleet, directed the assault on Tarawa for 30 hours without relief. By the time he was relieved, 75 percent of the island was under Marine control. (USMC)

This photo taken on Tarawa shows the grim sense of humor of some of the US troops following the bloody action to take the island. On Tarawa the Marines were forced to fight for every cave, trench, and strongpoint against a determined enemy who would not surrender. Still, 5,000 Marines took the island in four days of savage fighting. (NARA)

6th Marines at San Diego, went with them to Iceland until March 1943, and then joined the staff of the 2nd Marine Division. He served as Operations and Training Officer for the 2nd Division during the preparation of plans for the Tarawa invasion in Wellington, New Zealand.

Before communications with the fleet were severed, Col. Shoup sent the message, "Issue in doubt," and urgently requested reinforcements. Reinforcements could not, however, break through the coral reef and the withering Japanese fire.

Although severely shocked by an enemy artillery round exploding nearby, Col. Shoup marched along the beach, pistol in hand, rallying and chivvying the men huddled on the beach, leading groups of them inland to reinforce the pitifully thin line of men holding the precarious perimeter.

For 30 straight hours, Col. Shoup coordinated the Marines' relentless assault, despite a leg wound which had become infected. He sent his men where they were most needed, and despite grave danger of being dislodged, he so skillfully handled the offense that slowly, yard by yard, the situation began to change. Finally, on November 22, Col. Shoup was relieved by Colonel Edson Merritt, and was taken back to the fleet for medical attention. When he left, 75 percent of the Island was controlled by his Marines.

After Tarawa, Col. Shoup was promoted to Chief of Staff of the 2nd Division and finished the war in staff assignments. Promoted to Major General in 1955, General Shoup became, in short succession, the Commanding Officer of the First Marine Division and then the Third Marine Division. On January 1, 1960, he became the 22nd Commandant of the Marine Corps, at the rank of four-star general. Gen. Shoup retired in 1964, but remained an active and outspoken advocate until his death in 1983.

1st Lieutenant Alexander "Sandy" Bonnyman, Jr., USMCR

Throughout the second day on Tarawa, a trickle of reinforcements and much savage fighting allowed the troops ashore to push beyond their initial fragile beachhead. By the third day, 75 percent of the island was in US hands. Yet on the Marines' left flank, no progress had been made on Beach Red-3. The advance was held up by a huge camouflaged concrete bombproof directly in the Marines' path. All attempts to take it for the past two days had been unsuccessful. Unless this obstacle could be breached, the Marines would remain trapped in an exposed 10yd-deep perimeter, protected only by a low seawall of palm logs.

An unexpected hero came to the rescue, 1st Lieutenant Alexander "Sandy" Bonnyman, the executive officer of a shore party of engineers. Bonnyman, a native of Knoxville, Tennessee, was the son of Alexander Bonnyman, Sr., president of the Blue Diamond Coal Company. After attending Mrs Thackston's School in Knoxville, Young Alexander entered

Princeton in 1928, where he played guard on the school's football team. In 1930, he unexpectedly left Princeton in his sophomore year to go into business. He joined the Army Air Corps in 1932, but was dismissed for buzzing control towers. When war came, Bonnyman was exempt from conscription by virtue of occupation; he owned and operated copper mines which were considered necessary to the national defense. Despite his exemption from service, the news of Pearl Harbor so angered him that he enlisted in the Marines, leaving a wife and three daughters behind.

Although he had come ashore in a non-combat role, he clearly saw what the 8th Marines faced and took the job in hand. Although acting beyond the scope of his orders, Lt. Bonnyman was moved by the bloody stalemate. Almost immediately after landing, he took the initiative to organize and conduct parties of Marines across the fire-swept pier to the narrow stretch of beach behind the palm log seawall, where they could come to grips with the enemy. Later that day, with the Marines still pinned down behind the seawall, Lt. Bonnyman, again on his own initiative, crawled up several hundred yards towards the bombproof to examine it closely. Careful observation revealed air vents protruding from the roof. He was convinced that these vents were the key to destroying the bunker, and led forward a quickly patched together assault group of 21 men, armed with flame throwers, grenades, rifles, automatic weapons, and short fused sticks of TNT.

1st Lieutenant Alexander Bonnyman came ashore on Beach Red-3 on the third day of the battle for Tarawa. Although most of the island was taken by this time, the Marines at Red-3 were barely holding on to a 10yd-deep beach perimeter. Although sent ashore on a non-combat engineering mission, Lt. Bonnyman took charge and led a breakout attack against a huge Japanese concrete bombproof which blocked the Marines' progress. (USMC)

Lt. Bonnyman crawled 40yds and placed explosives at one of the entrances to the bombproof. He returned to lead his men over the sloping top of the bunker against fierce enemy fire. Marine flame throwers silenced several of the enemy machine gun emplacements guarding the bunker. Reaching the ventilators, flame thrower fuel was sprayed over the ventilators in addition to TNT charges being dropped down the vents. One of the blasts blew off the cover of an entrance, out of which burst a large group of Japanese Imperial Marines. At this time only Lt. Bonnyman and five of his men remained on the roof of the bombproof. While the others engaged in demolition duties, Lt. Bonnyman ran to the edge of the roof and rushed the enemy, armed only with an M-2 carbine. Firing as rapidly as possible, he killed several of the enemy but was shot dead just as reinforcements arrived from the other side of the bombproof.

In this bloodiest battle in the history of the Marine Corps to that date, the Marines moved forward with grim resolve, fighting for every cave and trench against a determined enemy who would not surrender. In the end, the Marines lost 1,000 dead and 2,200 wounded, while virtually the entire 4,800-man Japanese garrison was killed. Far from taking 100 years, 5,000 Marines had taken the impregnable island in just four days.

Lieutenant (junior grade) Albert Leroy David, USN

In June 1944, the Allies had turned the tide in the long and arduous Battle of the Atlantic against the U-boat menace. Longer-range aircraft had closed the mid-ocean gap, leaving no safe hunting grounds for the

In the bloodiest Marine Corps battle to that date, the attackers suffered 3,200 casualties out of 5,000 men, while almost all 4,800 Japanese invaders were killed. In later battles in the Pacific, the Japanese often left the beaches undefended and concentrated on resistance inland in prepared positions. However, at Tarawa, the Marines took terrific punishment on the beaches. At Beach Red-3, the Marines clung to a narrow strip of beach for several days in constant danger of being dislodged. (NARA)

U-boat wolf packs. At the same time, two other factors hastened the demise of Grossadmiral Karl Doenitz' elite force. The first great advances in technology (sonar in particular) made detection of submerged U-boats much more likely than in the past. The second element was the intelligence coup provided by the breaking of the German Armed Forces codes, which depended on the famous "Enigma" machine.

A special "Fleet", the 10th under Admiral Francis "Frog" Low, had no ships but was a shore establishment headquartered in Washington, D.C., concerned with the overall integration of intelligence and technology in the battle against the U-boat. As part of this effort, hunter-killer groups were instituted to go beyond the traditional passive convoy protection role into an active search-and-destroy capability. Task Group 22.3 was such a hunter-killer group, under the command of Captain Daniel Gallery, consisting of a "baby" aircraft carrier, the USS *Guadalcanal*, and 5 destroyer escorts: USS *Pillsbury, Chatelain, Pope, Flaherty*, and *Jenks*. On May 15, 1944, Task Group 22.3 began an antisubmarine warfare cruise, leaving from Norfolk, Virginia.

Task Group 22.3 was given intelligence from 10th Fleet providing details of U-boat activity obtained through decrypts of German Navy transmissions. In addition, Capt. Gallery had been provided with detailed drawings of the interior layout of German submarines, including the location of the controls and likely placement of scuttling charges. Capt.

Gallery was so anxious to capture a U-boat, he even staged rehearsals of boarding actions.

After searching unsuccessfully for a U-boat in the waters off Sierra Leone, Capt. Gallery broke off a search pattern and turned north towards Casablanca. Within minutes, the *Chatelain* made sonar contact just 800yds off her starboard bow. Commander Dudley Knox, captain of the *Chatelain*, radioed to the *Guadalcanal* to get clear while the destroyer escorts scrambled to close-in with the suspected U-boat. Just as the *Chatelain* fired her hedgehogs, the submarine fired a torpedo at the *Guadalcanal*. The *Chatelain* maneuvered to shield *Guadalcanal*, at the same time firing a torpedo towards the submarine. The German torpedo passed harmlessly underneath the *Chatelain*. *Guadalcanal* launched two aircraft to pinpoint the submarine's position, and the support ships pressed home depth charge attacks. When the damaged submarine surfaced, a blaze of concentrated small arms fire from the aircraft and the ships quickly forced the Germans to abandon ship.

As soon as Cdr Knox saw the German sailors jumping into the water, he dispatched the ship's whaleboat carrying a signalman armed with a Thompson submachine gun and a set of signal flags to the stricken submarine. The *Chatelain*'s signalman was soon joined by the *Pillsbury*'s whaleboat, carrying Lieutenant (junior grade) Albert David and his party of eight. Lt. David, born 42 years earlier in Maryville, Missouri, who later went on to win the Navy Cross with gold star, was about to earn his country's highest honor. The party boarded the enemy submarine, which was circling erratically on the water's surface. Upon entering the control room, they found that a seacock had been opened and the boat was filling with water. Aware that the sub could explode or sink, Lt. David and his men immediately searched for the open valve, at the same time pulling fuses from several scuttling charges. With additional men from the *Guadalcanal*, the open valves were found and the boat stabilized. Luckily, the Germans had not had time to set the scuttling charges. In the U-boat's radio room Lt. David found codebooks, equipment (including two "Enigma" cipher machines), and a mock-up of a new acoustic homing torpedo.

The U-boat turned out to be the U-505, commanded by Oberleutnant Harald Lange. Operating out of Lorient, France, the U-505 had sunk a total of 47,000 tons of Allied shipping over the preceding three years. She was a long-range sub whose area of operations centered on the South Atlantic, extending from Freetown, West Africa, to the Panama Canal, Colombia, and the Caribbean. Fifty-eight of the 59-man crew of the U-505 were rescued, only three wounded among them: the captain, the executive officer, and one rating.

While Lt. David and his men were securing U-505, the *Pillsbury* tried to come alongside to pass towing lines to the submarine, but was damaged by the U-boat's bow plane and had to withdraw for repairs. The U-505 had her own problems, sitting low in the water and down by

Lieutenant (junior grade) Albert David, serving aboard the destroyer escort USS *Pillsbury*, was part of antisubmarine Task Group 22.3 when the German submarine U-505 surfaced after a depth charge attack off the west coast of Africa. As the crew abandoned ship, Lt. David went with eight men in a whale boat to seize the U-boat before it could be scuttled. (Photograph courtesy of Home of Heroes.)

the stern. Eventually, the *Guadalcanal* was able to bring the submarine under tow, but the flooding had to be corrected or the U-505 would sink. By great ingenuity a solution was found: the diesel engines were disconnected, allowing the propellers to turn as the boat was towed through the water. The propellers would then turn the shafts and by setting the switches to recharge, the batteries' charges could be replenished. Once electrical power was available, the sub's own pumps could bail out the water. After three days, a US Navy tug, the *Abnaki*, took U-505 in tow for the remainder of the trip to Port Royal Bay, Bermuda, arriving on June 19, 1944.

The major intelligence prize was the capture of the codebooks, which yielded a partial solution to the problem of the special naval code which gave more precise locations of German U-boats than those available from the "Enigma" decrypts. The captured "Enigma" machines proved something of an embarrassment, however, since the Allies already had access to this equipment for some time, but they couldn't allow the Germans to learn of this fact. Accordingly, the entire episode had to be kept secret until the end of the war. Some portions remained secret for a generation. In the early 1980s, the wartime U-boat commander, Admiral Doenitz, still believed that the German naval code had never been compromised.

For his part in saving the U-505, Lt. David was awarded the Medal of Honor, and Task Group 22.3 was awarded a presidential unit citation for capturing an enemy warship on the high seas, the first time an American ship had done so since 1815.

After the war, U-505 was slated to be destroyed by gunnery and torpedo practice, but the people of Chicago, Illinois, raised $250,000 to

continued on page 41

U-505 was the first vessel to be captured by US naval forces since the War of 1812. This rare photograph shows the considerable topside damage which the submarine had suffered during the attack preceding the capture. The submarine was towed back to Bermuda, but U-505's intact capture was to remain a strict secret until the end of the war. (US Navy)

The US Navy and USMC Medal of Honor
The highest award for bravery that the United States can bestow on a member of its military, the Medal of Honor is a simple, yet elegant design that consists of a bronze five-pointed star suspended by an anchor device from a watered blue silk ribbon. The center theme on the star is the figure of Columbia dressed as Minerva defeating the figure of Discord. The medal shown was awarded to Chief Water Tender Peter Tomich (see plate commentary for details).

B

Commander Cassin Young; USS *Vestal*,
Pearl Harbor, December 7, 1941

Commander Richard Antrim; Makassar, April 1942

C

First Lieutenant Jefferson DeBlanc; VMF-112, 1942

D

Commander Richard O'Kane;
USS *Tang*, October 24, 1944

E

Hospital Apprentice 1st Class
Robert Eugene Bush; Okinawa,
May 2, 1945

F

Boatswain's Mate 2nd Class Owen Francis Hammerberg;
Pearl Harbor, February 17, 1945

Sergeant "Manila" John Basilone; Lunga Ridge, Guadalcanal, October, 1942

house the U-boat in the Chicago Museum of Science and Industry. In 1954, U-505 was put on display in Chicago as a permanent war memorial, and is today a registered National Historic Landmark.

Lieutenant-Commander David McCampbell, USN

By mid-1944, the Japanese decided to conduct a naval showdown in the Philippine Islands area, where the US forces were at a disadvantage being far from their supply lines. Early on June 19, 1944, the Japanese began a series of four large carrier raids, each consisting of over 300 aircraft launched against the American Fifth Fleet, then engaged in the invasion of Saipan. Among the planes that met these huge forces were those of VF-15, under its new commander, David McCampbell.

McCampbell, born in Bessemer, Alabama, in 1910, graduated from the Naval Academy in 1933. McCampbell's naval career, however, was almost over before it had begun. Due to a lack of funding during the Depression, McCampbell, along with many other new Academy graduates (including John Bulkeley, whose story is told in this book) was released from the Navy upon graduation. In June 1934, however, McCampbell was recalled to service, commissioned, and joined the fleet as a gunnery officer aboard the cruiser USS *Portland*. His flying career began after graduating at NAS Pensacola as an aviator in 1938.

When the United States entered World War II, Lt. McCampbell was assigned as the Landing Signals Officer (LSO) aboard the aircraft carrier USS *Wasp*. An LSO, often referred to as "Paddles", was the officer responsible for the safe landing of all aircraft. Stationed at the end of the carrier's flight deck, he signaled with large paddles to direct aircraft in for a safe landing.

Promoted to the rank of Lieutenant-Commander in the spring of 1944, McCampbell was at last given a flying assignment: command of the new fighter squadron VF-15 assigned to the aircraft carrier USS *Essex*. He was at long last a rookie aviator at the age of 34. He did not wait long to make a reputation: in the month following his first kill on May 19, he shot down a total of five Japanese aircraft.

As the massive Japanese raids of June 19, 1944, moved against the invasion fleet at Saipan, Lt Cdr McCampbell's part began at approximately 1100 when 12 VF-15 fighters intercepted a flight of Aichi D4 "Judy" dive-bombers 60 miles out, headed for the American carriers. The Japanese flew in a tight defensive formation with interlocking fields of fire. McCampbell quickly assessed the situation and attacked, first hitting one side of the formation and then the other. VF-15 pilots shot down about half of the attacking Japanese planes, with McCampbell accounting for five.

Later in the day, during the fourth and largest Japanese attack of the battle, McCampbell led another sortie against the Japanese. After

Prior to his Pacific service, then Lieutenant David McCampbell served as a Landing Signals Officer. Commander McCampbell was the US Navy top ace in the Second World War with 34 combat victories. (US Navy)

McCampbell's personal aircraft, *Minsi III*, is given the once-over by his crew chief and ground crew aboard the USS *Essex*, CV-9, in 1944. (US Navy)

shooting down another Zero fighter, he became separated from the rest of his squad. Alone and deep in enemy territory approaching the nearby island of Guam, McCampbell caught sight of an American scout plane, harassed by two attacking Japanese fighters, that was attempting to rescue downed American pilots. Diving to the rescue, McCampbell quickly shot down one of the Zeros, which burst into flames and crashed into the ocean. The second Zero was brought down by another VF-15 pilot, who had also observed the disturbance between the American rescue plane and the Japanese fighters.

For McCampbell, this one day's action resulted in seven victories and one probable, bringing his total to 12. Losses among the Japanese were so heavy that this action became known as the "Mariana's Turkey Shoot". Following this, McCampbell was ordered by his commander not to take any more unnecessary risks as Air Group commander.

However, a chance for further action came for McCampbell on October 24, 1944, when his squadron took on an in-coming Japanese attack force of 60 aircraft. When the action was over, McCampbell and his wingman had accounted for 15 planes between them, credit for nine going to McCampbell.

Promoted to full Commander, McCampbell, the US Navy's top-scoring ace of the war with a final count of 34 planes, was presented with the Medal of Honor for the two Battles of the Philippine Sea in a White House ceremony on January 10, 1945. Following the war, McCampbell remained in the Navy rising to the rank of Captain, with a list of commands including that of the Fleet Oiler USS *Severn* and the aircraft carrier USS *Bon Homme Richard*. Captain McCampbell retired from the service in 1964. He passed away in 1996, and is buried at Arlington National Cemetery.

Private First Class Harold Christ Agerholm, USMCR

After Tarawa, the Joint Chiefs of Staff determined that the primary objective for 1944 would be the establishing of a strategic air base from which to launch the new B-29 Superfortresses on bombing campaigns against the Japanese home islands. Luzon, Formosa, and even the China coast itself were considered, but Saipan, in the Mariana Islands, was chosen, primarily because of its location, 1,200 miles from Tokyo and 1,500 miles from Manila.

Saipan was an island some 85 square miles in size and consisted of a mixture of steep ravines, rocky hills, jungles, and swamps; ideal terrain for a tenacious Japanese defense. The Japanese defenders of the island consisted of some 25,000 army personnel under the command of Lieutenant-General Hideyoshi Obata of the 31st Army and some 6,000

Navy personnel consisting of Marines and aviators under the command of Vice Admiral Chuichi Nagumo. Characteristically, the Japanese defenders of Saipan suffered from command and control problems between the Army and the Navy personnel, since each component had its own commander. This lack of unity of command was to prove a fatal flaw in the Japanese defense of Saipan.

On the American side, the forces chosen for the attack were the 2nd Marine Division under the command of General Thomas E. Watson, the 4th Marine Division under General Harry Schmidt, and the Army's 27th Infantry Division, commanded by General Ralph C. Smith, approximately 67,000 troops in all. Marine General Holland "Howling Mad" Smith was in overall command of the operation.

Among the regiments of the 2nd Marine Division was the 10th Marines, in whose ranks was a 19-year-old private first class who would soon add luster to its name. Harold Agerholm, a native of Racine, Wisconsin, was born on January 29, 1925. He enlisted in the United States Marine Corps in July 1942 and was subsequently assigned to the 4th Battalion, 10th Marine Regiment of the 2nd Marine Division as battery storekeeper for the mortar section. Pfc. Agerholm had participated in the Marine assault on Tarawa in November, 1943, and, along with the rest of the 2nd Marine Division, had been sent back to Hawaii to rest and recuperate before going on the invasion of Saipan.

Private First Class Harold Agerholm is shown wearing the dark green wool enlisted service dress uniform worn by most Marines during the war, in place of the more formal dress blue uniform. (USMC)

General Smith's plans for the invasion called for the Marines to land on a two-mile stretch of land on the western side of the island, near the town of Charan Kanoa. Amphibious tractors and tanks were to move inland and establish a defensive perimeter which Marine riflemen would then consolidate. Almost from the first, the plan began to unravel as a gap developed in the Marine beachhead due to uneven Japanese resistance and the vulnerability of the amphibious tractors, which proved unable to establish a defensive perimeter.

Pfc. Agerholm and his detachment of the 10th Marines went ashore on the third day and participated in the assault against Mount Tapotchau, the highest point on the island. Eventually, after hard fighting, the enemy position on Tapotchau was taken on July 5, 1944. With the Marines stretched to the limit, the Japanese launched a Banzai charge against the 27th Division that overwhelmed two battalions and allowed the Japanese to break through the Army positions and threaten the beachhead. The 2nd Marines, in reserve, had to be called in to throw back the rampaging Japanese and restore the line. During the attack and counterattacks, casualties for both sides were extremely heavy, placing a strain on the ability of medical personnel to evacuate wounded men to the beach.

Pfc. Agerholm located an abandoned ambulance jeep and made repeated trips under heavy fire to evacuate wounded personnel to the

On the day following the Marine landings on Saipan, they were reinforced by US Army troops from the 27th Infantry Division. In this official Army photograph, we see men of the 27th wade ashore from Navy LSTs waiting offshore at Saipan's barrier reef. (NARA)

beach, eventually saving 45 men during a three-hour period. Later, noticing two wounded Marines lying beyond the lines, Pfc. Agerholm dashed out to pull them back to safety but was cut down by enemy sniper fire. For his gallant and selfless action, Pfc. Harold Agerholm was awarded the Medal of Honor, which was presented to his mother, at her request, in an unusual private ceremony.

Captain Louis Hugh Wilson, Jr., USMC

As the Marines fought for Saipan, another island in the group, Guam, was also a target of prime importance as an air base to accommodate the new B-29 bombers. The war strategists considered the island the best possible advance base against both the Philippines and the Japanese home islands due to its relatively large size (at 228 square miles it was three times larger than Saipan) and because it was within B-29 range of both the Japanese mainland and the Philippines.

The invasion was launched by the 3rd Marine Division on July 21, 1944. It was the task of 2nd Battalion, 9th Marines to land on Blue Beach, at the extreme right flank of the 3rd Marine Division, with the objective of seizing the ridges just forward of the beaches and driving west to Apra Harbor to link up with other Marines forces from the 1st Provisional Marine Brigade.

Captain Louis Wilson, Jr., in command of Company F, 2nd Battalion, 9th Marines, came ashore on July 21, 1944, with the assault waves of the 3rd Marine Division. Captain Wilson, a native of Brandon, Mississippi, was born on February 11, 1920, enlisted in the US Marine Corps in 1941, and was assigned to the officer candidate program. He was commissioned as a second lieutenant in November 1941, and was assigned to the 2nd Battalion of the 9th Marine Regiment and sent overseas. He saw action at Guadalcanal, Efate, and Bougainville.

Now on Guam, crossing the reefs in amphibious tractors, the 9th Marines advanced inland, the 3rd Battalion leading the way, followed by the 2nd, with the 1st Battalion being held in reserve. Just as they were reaching their objectives, heavy Japanese resistance caused the advance to bog down. Nevertheless, over the next two days, Capt. Wilson's battalion gradually expanded its lodgment area and even managed to recapture the US Navy Yard at Piti.

On July 25, the 2nd Battalion was ordered to spearhead an attack on Japanese positions on Fonte Hill. Advancing some 300yds under heavy Japanese machine gun fire, the battalion succeeded in taking its objective. Capt. Wilson, finding himself the senior officer, began to organize his men for the inevitable counterattack. During the course of the night, Capt. Wilson was wounded three times in five hours, but the defensive situation was so serious, under constant threat of Banzai charges, that Capt. Wilson felt compelled to stay with his command. At one point, seeing a wounded Marine lying helpless some 50yds from their lines, Capt. Wilson, at great risk to his own life, dashed forward to carry the fallen man back.

The night of July 25–26 saw some of the heaviest Banzai charges of the war and earned the Fonte plateau the nickname "Banzai Ridge". When the action was over, the bodies of some 950 enemy soldiers

Captain Louis Wilson (shown as a Major in this photograph) was typical of the tough no-nonsense officers who commanded both the respect of their men and the enemy during the island-hopping campaigns in the Pacific. (USMC)

In this 1944 photograph, two US officers plant the first American flag on the beach at Guam. In the background, troops come ashore in an amphibious tractor. (NARA)

Unlike the jungle fighting that was to characterize much of the fighting in the island-hopping campaign, the fighting on Guam featured house-to-house clearing, as typified by this 3rd Division soldier moving to check the second story of this house in Guam. (NARA)

sprawled along the 2nd Battalion's front, bearing mute witness to the fierceness of the Japanese attack. During ten hours, Capt. Wilson and his men held their own in some of the most determined hand-to-hand fighting of the Pacific campaign and suffered nearly 50 percent casualties as a result.

On the next morning, July 26, Capt. Wilson organized a patrol of 17 men to take the high ground in front of his company's defensive position. Advancing into the teeth of severe enemy machine gun and mortar fire which killed or wounded 13 of his men, Capt. Wilson boldly seized the high ground and held the position against heavy odds.

Following the action on Fonte Hill, Capt. Wilson was evacuated to the US until the end of the war. After the war, Wilson remained in the Marine Corps, making brigadier general in 1966, and receiving his fourth star as Commandant of the Corps in 1975. He retired in 1979, after 38 years of service, and now lives in California.

Commander Richard Hetherington O'Kane, USN

With the struggle to retake the Philippines beginning in October 1944, most of the US Navy's submarine efforts were directed to stop the flow of supplies and reinforcements to the Japanese defenders in the Philippines. US Navy subs focused on the East China Sea, the Formosa Straits, the Luzon Strait, the South China Sea and Manila Bay. Operations in the shallow waters of the China Sea were extremely hazardous for US submarines due to the ease of detection by Japanese surface forces equipped with sonar.

The USS *Tang*, SS-306, a new "Balao" class submarine, joined the submarine offensive in the Western Pacific in early 1944. While under construction at Mare Island Navy Yard in California in July 1943, the *Tang* received a veteran submarine officer as skipper, Commander Richard H. O'Kane. Thirty-two-year-old Cdr O'Kane, a 1934 graduate of the Naval Academy, had served on both cruisers and destroyers prior to joining the submarine force in 1938. Before being given the *Tang*, Cdr O'Kane had served as executive officer of USS *Wahoo*, under the command of Cdr Dudley "Mush" Morton, one of the most famous and aggressive submarine commanders of World War II. Here, Cdr O'Kane honed his skills under the tutelage of a submarine force legend during five war patrols.

The *Tang*, commissioned in October 1943, joined the Pacific fleet in Hawaii in January 1944. Although the *Tang* was not destined to have a long career as a warship, during the year that she was in service her skipper, Cdr O'Kane, became one of the highest-scoring submarine aces of the war, with a total of 227,800 tons of Japanese shipping sunk.

The *Tang*'s penchant for success manifested early. On her first five-week patrol in 1944, the *Tang* sank five Japanese vessels off the Caroline and Mariana islands, a total of 22,000 tons. The second patrol, at the end of April 1944, saw the *Tang* on lifeguard duty in support of a large air raid on Truk, during which 22 downed fliers were rescued. On the next five-week patrol in the East China Sea, she set a record: ten Japanese vessels sunk, with a total tonnage of 39,100. On the fourth patrol in Japanese home waters, the *Tang* accounted for two more vessels, totaling 11,500 tons.

Embarking on her fifth war patrol late in September 1944, the *Tang* arrived at the Formosa Strait on October 10. The area in and around the island of Formosa proved a difficult place for submarines because of large areas of shallow water. If caught unaware, a submarine could only dive to a minimum depth to avoid attack, thus, greatly increasing the risk of destruction. In addition to the dangers posed by enemy surface vessels, the Japanese set extensive mine fields around the China coast to protect its convoy routes from marauding submarines.

On the night of October 22–23, 1944, the *Tang* picked up on radar a Japanese convoy of six ships. Cdr O'Kane, determined to attack this convoy on the surface, carefully maneuvered the *Tang* in front of the convoy's route and prepared to penetrate the escort screen. While the Japanese escorts scanned the horizon, Cdr O'Kane handled the *Tang* in such a way to make her silhouette appear as small as possible to the Japanese ships until he could bring his sub inside the convoy itself. Picking out the *Toun Maru* as his target, Cdr O'Kane launched a torpedo attack from close range. One torpedo set the *Toun Maru* afire while two others sank her convoy mate, the *Tatsuju Maru*. In the chaos that followed, another Japanese vessel, the *Wakatake Maru*, sighted the *Tang* and attempted to ram her. As Cdr O'Kane said, "[i]t was really a thriller diller, with the Tang barely getting on the inside of his turning circle and saving the stern with a full left rudder in the last seconds."

Cdr O'Kane ordered the bridge cleared and was starting to crash dive when he suddenly saw that his erstwhile attacker had collided with another Japanese vessel. With decks awash, Cdr O'Kane ordered two more torpedoes to be fired at the entangled ships. With phenomenal accuracy, both torpedoes struck their targets. In the end, the *Tang* had penetrated a screen of warships around a heavily defended convoy and sunk four of the six vessels in the convoy. For this action Cdr O'Kane was awarded the Medal of Honor, but he would have to wait for war's end to receive it.

Twenty-four hours later, on the night of October 24–25, 1944, the *Tang*'s luck ran out. While attacking another convoy, the *Tang* was struck in the stern by one of her own errant torpedoes and sank rapidly to the bottom. Only nine members of the crew, including Cdr O'Kane, survived, but they spent the rest of the war in a Japanese prisoner of war camp.

Following the war and a lengthy convalescence, Cdr O'Kane received the Medal of Honor from President Truman in a White House

A Navy photograph of an oil painting by Commander Albert K. Murray showing Cdr O'Kane aboard the USS *Tang* in 1944. (US Navy)

Commander Richard O'Kane
receives the Congressional
Medal of Honor from President
Harry S. Truman in a ceremony
conducted following his release
from a Naval hospital. At the time
of his liberation from a Japanese
prison camp, Cdr O'Kane
weighed only 88lbs and was
not expected to live. (US Navy)

ceremony. Cdr O'Kane, the fiery warhorse, remained in the post-war Navy, but found adjustment to peacetime difficult. After a series of routine jobs, he retired from the service in 1957, with the rank of Captain. He wrote two books based on his experiences, *Wahoo* and *Clear the Bridge*. He died in 1994 in Petaluma, California, from complications associated with pneumonia. His body rests at Arlington National Cemetery.

Commander Eugene Bennett Fluckey, USN

Like the *Tang*, the USS *Barb*, SS-220, was sent to the Formosa Strait in early 1945 to attack the supply lines supporting Japanese action against US forces in the Philippines. Also like the *Tang*, the *Barb* was the focus for an action of supreme heroism.

In late 1943, the *Barb*, a veteran of six successful war patrols, received a new commanding officer, Cdr Eugene Fluckey. Born in Washington, D.C., in 1913, "Gene" Fluckey entered the Naval Academy in 1935, and upon graduation served two years in the surface fleet before transferring to the submarine service in 1938. When America entered the war in 1941, Lieutenant Fluckey was serving aboard the USS *Bonita*, a prewar "B" class sub which had been ordered to the Pacific. There Fluckey sailed on five war patrols from December 1941 to August 1942, before returning home to attend postgraduate school in engineering.

Late in 1943, Lieutenant-Commander Fluckey transferred to the *Barb* and sailed aboard her for one war patrol before assuming command in April, 1944. After this, the *Barb*'s seventh war patrol, Cdr Fluckey assumed charge and in the course of five subsequent war patrols, he was credited with sinking 95,630 tons of Japanese shipping. On the *Barb*'s eleventh war patrol, the fourth with Cdr Fluckey in charge, she was ordered into the China Sea.

For her eleventh war patrol, the *Barb* and her pack mates, USS *Picuda* and USS *Queenfish*, were to act "as the cork in the bottle" to deny Japanese shipping use of the Formosa Strait. They entered the China Sea on January 3, 1945, proceeded north, parallel to the China coast, and took up station, with the *Barb* as the "in-shore" boat.

On January 8, the *Barb*, *Picuda*, and *Queenfish* encountered a Japanese convoy of eight large merchant ships under the protection of four frigates and four smaller patrol craft. In the ensuing attack, torpedoes from Cdr Fluckey's subs were responsible for sinking four of the convoy's merchant ships.

The weeks following the attack on the convoy were fraught with frustration for the crew of the *Barb*: there were no enemy vessels to be found. All that changed on the night of January 22, when the *Barb* caught sight of a large Japanese convoy in the anchorage of Namkwan, China. Cdr Fluckey decided to attack the convoy from the surface due to low visibility and the shallow water of the harbor. At 0300 the *Barb* slipped past the Japanese escort that was guarding the entrance to the anchorage and began her run on the convoy. Cdr Fluckey fired his bow torpedoes at the densely packed convoy from a range of 4,000yds then swung around to fire a parting shot. In moments, the night erupted in fire and chaos as the *Barb's* torpedoes struck their targets, sinking four ships and damaging three others in a devastating volley.

With the convoy in ruins, the *Barb* began a wild surface dash for the safety of deep water. With a Japanese frigate in hot pursuit, Cdr Fluckey ordered his sub to emergency power and steered towards the rocks and shoals. Racing along at 23 knots, the *Barb* suddenly made radar contact with a group of Chinese junks in the darkness. As the submarine passed through them, the Japanese frigate opened fire. Rather than hitting the *Barb,* the Japanese hit the junks. By 0500 the *Barb* reached deep water and evaded pursuit. For this feat, Cdr Fluckey received the Medal of Honor.

Before the war ended, Cdr Fluckey made one more successful patrol aboard the *Barb.* Following the war he remained in the Silent Service, commanding two more submarines, USS *Dogfish* and USS *Halbeak*, and the submarine tender USS *Sperry.* From 1964 to 1966 Cdr Fluckey acted as Commander Submarines, Pacific Fleet, and retired from the Navy in 1972 after 37 years of service, with the rank of Rear Admiral. He currently resides in Annapolis, Maryland.

Corporal Tony Stein, USMCR

After taking Tinian, Saipan, and Guam, American strategy turned northeast to Iwo Jima, the southernmost island in a 700-mile chain which reached all the way to Japan. Iwo Jima boasted two Japanese airbases which were being used to harass newly established US bases on Saipan, Tinian, and Guam. Even more important than removing this menace, American airbases on Iwo Jima would permit, for the first time, fighter escort for B-29 bomber raids on the Japanese mainland. Once again, the Marines were called to make the assault, the first on Japanese territory itself.

The V Amphibious Corps, under the command of General Harry Schmidt, consisting of the 3rd, 4th, and 5th Marine Divisions, some 74,000 men in all, was to be committed to the assault of the island, code-named DETACHMENT. Landing beaches were chosen on the eastern side of Iwo Jima in a two mile stretch of land that ran from the base of Mount Suribachi, at the southern tip of the island, to East Boat Basin. The 5th Division, to which Corporal Tony Stein's outfit belonged, was assigned a 550yd section of beach known as "Green Beach", located at the foot of Mount Suribachi.

On February 19, 1945, the Marines began their effort to wrest the island from the Japanese by storming ashore in a great amphibious assault. Among the invaders was Corporal Stein, Company A, 1st Battalion, 28th Marine Regiment attached to the 5th Marine Division.

Commander Eugene "Lucky" Fluckey is shown on the deck of the USS *Barb* after being awarded the Navy Cross after his eighth war patrol. (US Navy)

Corporal Tony Stein was almost unable to go to war because of his work in a defense plant as a tool and die maker. Later in Hawaii, he would use these skills to make a personal weapon that he called a stinger from an air-cooled .30-cal. machine gun. (USMC photograph)

Stein, a 23-year-old from Dayton, Ohio, had enlisted in the US Marine Corps in 1942 and joined the Marine Raiders after basic training. He saw action at Guadalcanal and Bougainville, where he managed to shoot five Japanese snipers in one day. After the Raiders were disbanded in 1944, Stein transferred to the 5th Marine Division at Camp Pendleton, California. There he was promoted to Corporal and assistant squad leader in Company A, 1st Battalion, 28th Marine Regiment, a unit that was to take part in the February 1945 invasion of Iwo Jima.

Once ashore, Cpl. Stein's company was to establish themselves on the beach and begin to work inland in an attempt to cut Mount Suribachi off from the rest of the Japanese garrison. According to Cpl. Stein's medal citation, "The first man of his unit to be on station after hitting the beach in the initial assault, Cpl. Stein, armed with a personally improvised aircraft-type weapon, provided rapid covering fire as the remainder of his platoon moved into position."

This improvised weapon was a .30-cal. aircraft machine gun (no doubt irregularly obtained) that the Corporal had modified so that he could move around reasonably freely firing from the hip while on the move.

As the 1st Battalion began its push across the base of Mount Suribachi, they ran headlong into the heavily entrenched positions defended by the Japanese 312th Independent Infantry Battalion. These positions were sited as a defense in-depth consisting of machine gun pillboxes supported by mortars. Again Corporal Stein was equal to the situation:

When his comrades were stalled by a concentrated machine gun and mortar barrage, he gallantly stood upright and exposed himself to the enemy's view, whereby drawing the hostile fire to his own person and enabling him to observe the location of the furiously blazing hostile guns. Determined to neutralize the strategically placed weapons, he boldly charged enemy pillboxes one by one and succeeded in killing 20 of the enemy during the furious single-handed charge.

All through the long afternoon, Corporal Stein made eight trips back to the beach for ammunition for his weapon, removing his shoes and helmet at one point in order to move faster. On each trip he insisted upon taking a wounded man back to the beach with him. By the end of the first day and after much hard fighting, the first battalion managed to cut off Mount Suribachi from the rest of Iwo Jima. For his heroism that day, Corporal Stein was awarded the Medal of Honor.

Over the next four days, the 28th Regiment was involved in the taking of Mt. Suribachi itself. On February 23, a small patrol of 40 Marines arrived at the summit, where they hurriedly raised an American flag, soon replaced by a larger one. The famous photograph of the raising of this second flag on Mt. Suribachi has provided an enduring icon for the bravery of Marines everywhere.

American troops finally clawed their way to the top of Mt. Suribachi on Iwo Jima after fierce fighting. Here a US Marine looks down from the summit over Green Beach to the right where Corporal Tony Stein and the rest of his outfit landed on the first day of the invasion. (NARA)

Corporal Tony Stein started out as a parachute-qualified Marine Raider, but at Bougainville earned the reputation as a sniper hunter. These Raiders are photographed in the jungle at the end of the Bougainville campaign. (NARA)

During World War II, as before and since, the Navy provided all medical personnel for the Marine Corps. Comparable to the Army "medics", the Navy "corpsmen" went through Marine Corps weapons training and were closely integrated into the Marine ground units. Although the official corpsman's uniform bore Navy insignia, it was not uncommon for corpsmen to wear USMC insignia, as shown in this picture of Pharmacist's Mate 1st Class Francis Pierce. (USMC)

With the fall of Suribachi, the 5th Marine Division began a methodical advance up the west coast of the island until reaching Hill 362A, a rough area dominated by Japanese defensive positions. Corporal Stein, who had been evacuated to a hospital ship for treatment of wounds received on Mount Suribachi, learned of heavy losses suffered at Hill 362A, left the hospital ship, and made his way back to his men. Leading a patrol of 19 men to investigate a machine gun that had his company pinned down, Stein was killed by a sniper on March 1, less than two weeks after the action for which he would receive the Medal of Honor. In 1972, the Navy commissioned a frigate of the "Knox" Class, FF-1065, USS *Stein*, in honor of this Marine hero of Iwo Jima.

Pharmacist's Mate 1st Class Francis J. Pierce, USN

Medical personnel were an indispensable presence on all the battlefields of the war, but nowhere did they have more scope for their services than in the hard-fought battles of the Pacific Campaign. The call for "Corpsman!" was heard all over the Pacific, anywhere Marines fought and died.

Francis Pierce, Pharmacist's Mate 1st Class, was one of their number. Enlisting in the Navy on the day Pearl Harbor was attacked, he trained in first-aid and pharmacy and was assigned to the 4th Marine Division. By 1945, he had already participated in landings on Saipan and Tinian before heading to Iwo Jima with the 2nd Battalion, 24th Marines.

Pierce's style as a corpsman was far from traditional. Since the Japanese had rejected the Geneva Convention as antithetical to the Bushido tradition, they treated medical personnel on the battlefield no differently to combatants. Accordingly, Pierce had received full Marine rifleman training in addition to his medical training, and he used this skill aggressively in carrying out his corpsman's duties. Armed with a Thompson submachine gun, Pierce would approach a wounded Marine with gun blazing to keep the enemies' heads down. Agressiveness, combined with thorough preparation, allowed him to survive some of the hardest fighting of the Pacific War unwounded for almost an entire month. He memorized the terrain he covered and always carried a map, noting the location of enemy positions as he went about ministering to the wounded. This map, annotated with areas where he had previously received fire, allowed him to plot relatively safe routes to the wounded he rescued. In this way, he was regularly able to traverse the areas of hottest fighting without injury for an incredible 25 days.

On March 15, 1945, Corpsman Pierce, along with a group of corpsmen and stretcher bearers, went out to rescue two wounded Marines when they were caught in a savage cross-fire. One corpsman and two stretcher bearers were wounded. Pierce took charge and covered the evacuation of three of the five wounded by exposing himself

to draw fire. Once that party was safe, he began to stanch the bleeding of one of the two remaining casualties when a Japanese sniper fired at them from 20yds, wounding one of Corpsman Pierce's patients again. Once more, he exposed himself and beat the sniper to the draw, killing him with the last of his ammunition. He then carried the twice-wounded Marine 200ft through open terrain under extremely heavy rifle fire. Oblivious to the warnings of his superiors, he returned unarmed the way he had come and rescued the last wounded man, carrying him to safety through the gauntlet of Japanese fire.

The next day, Corpsman Pierce identified a snipers' nest on his map and led a patrol to wipe it out. The mission was successful but he was seriously wounded while giving aid to a wounded Marine. Refusing treatment for himself, he explained to the others how to tend to the wounded man, at the same time covering the group with protective fire.

Corpsman Pierce left the Navy in December 1945, with the Navy Cross and the Silver Star, and on June 25, 1946, President Truman presented him with the Medal of Honor. Pierce returned to Iowa, but soon moved to Grand Rapids, Michigan, here he married and started a career with the Grand Rapids Police Department. He also joined the Michigan National Guard in 1949 and was honorably discharged as a 2nd Lieutenant. He rose to the rank of Deputy Police Chief in Grand Rapids, where he succumbed to cancer in 1986 at the age of 62.

Lieutenant-Commander (Chaplain Corps) Joseph O'Callahan, USNR

In spring 1945, the largest invasion fleet yet assembled in the Pacific war moved across the Pacific Ocean towards a rendezvous in the Ryukyu Islands for what would prove to be the final battle of World War II. The objective was to invade the island of Okinawa, Operation ICEBERG. The magnitude of the operation, however, was dwarfed at the time by the specter of the ultimate battle to come in a few months, the invasion of the Japanese mainland itself. A successful operation on Okinawa could place an American airfield that would support a force of nearly 800 aircraft within medium bomber range of Kyushu (350 miles) and Tokyo (750 miles) and complete preparations for the projected invasion of Japan.

The proximity to Japan gave Okinawa its strategic importance but likewise placed the proposed invasion area well within range of Japanese aircraft operating from the Japanese mainland.

Admiral Marc Mitscher's Task Force 58, which included the 27,000-ton "Essex" class aircraft carrier USS *Franklin*, had been assigned to attack airfields on mainland Japan in support of the coming assault on Okinawa, set for Easter Sunday, April 1, 1945. On March 19, the *Franklin*'s aircraft attacked Japanese naval bases in the Inland Sea. Not long afterward, the *Franklin* was hit twice by a single Japanese bomber which had penetrated the outer defenses of the task force. The bomber

A Roman Catholic priest, Father Joseph O'Callahan was a mathematics professor at Holy Cross College before the war. At the outbreak of war, Father O'Callahan learned that his sister, a missionary in the Philippines, had been taken prisoner by the Japanese and he wished to find out first-hand what had happened to her. He was the first military chaplain ever to receive the nation's highest award for combat gallantry, which he earned on the burning deck of the USS *Franklin* on March 19, 1945, in the waters off Okinawa. Here Father O'Callahan wears the service dress gray uniform authorized to replace the older khaki uniform in 1942. (US Navy)

came out of a cloud bank at an altitude of 75ft and dropped a 500lb armor-piercing bomb onto the *Franklin's* flight deck, returned for another pass, and dropped a second bomb on the aft portion of the deck. The first bomb penetrated to the hangar deck, igniting massive fires. The second bomb penetrated the flight deck and started fires which soon set off stored ammunition, bombs, and rockets. The *Franklin* was left dead in the water: a flaming inferno. The death toll would eventually reach 832.

Early that morning, the chaplain of the *Franklin* had already broadcast over the ship's loudspeaker a service of absolution in anticipation of his ship's launching an air strike. The chaplain was Father Joseph O'Callahan, and he had followed an unusually academic apprenticeship for a Navy chaplain. Born in 1905 in Roxbury, Massachusetts, he had entered the Society of Jesus after attending high school at Boston College High School. In 1929, he completed a degree in philosophy at Weston College and joined the Boston College physics faculty. Continuing with his religious vocation, Father O'Callahan was ordained a Roman Catholic priest in 1934. He completed postgraduate work at Georgetown University and then returned to teaching, first at Weston College and then, in 1938, at Holy Cross College, where he was made head of the Mathematics Department in 1940. To the surprise of everyone who knew him, Father O'Callahan applied to the Navy Chaplain's Corps in 1940 and was commissioned a Lieutenant junior grade the same year. He was first assigned to the Naval Air Station, Pensacola, Florida, and then to the aircraft carrier USS *Ranger*, where he remained until March 1945, when he was transferred to the USS *Franklin*.

Father O'Callahan was having his breakfast that morning in the wardroom when the ship was rocked by multiple explosions. Everyone immediately dove under the tables in an instinctive attempt to protect themselves from flying debris. For the second time that morning, Father O'Callahan gave absolution to those around him.

Sensing that the situation was serious, Father O'Callahan returned to his stateroom to recover his religious supplies, especially the holy oil used in the administration of last rites. He headed first to some of the aviators' quarters, where he found many wounded and dying in need of his services. Spending a few precious minutes with each man in need, Father O'Callahan brought what comfort he could in that scene of fear and suffering.

Father O'Callahan next went to the hangar deck, but soon realized that no one could be alive in the ferocious fire raging there. He made his way topside to the flight deck. Seeing devastation everywhere, Father O'Callahan soon realized that he was the only officer in sight, and unless quick action was taken, the *Franklin* would be lost. He gave aid and direction to the firefighting crews battling multiple

The USS *Franklin* was struck by a kamikaze attack on March 14, 1945, and set afire. This official Navy photograph shows some of the damage caused by two Japanese 500lb bombs. One bomb pierced the flight deck and started a fire which threatened to engulf stores of ordnance including bombs and rockets. Finding himself the only officer in sight, Father O'Callahan organized parties to fight the fires and others to throw ordnance overboard before the fire could reach them. (US Navy)

blazes. Fire was threatening some ammunition for the 5in. guns, so he organized and led a group to throw the rapidly heating shells overboard.

Father O'Callahan alternated between fighting fires and ministering to the wounded all through the day and into the night. Due to his efforts, and those of the remaining crew, the *Franklin* survived with the distinction of being the most heavily damaged US Navy vessel still to remain afloat. Father O'Callahan had little time to rest for several days after the immediate danger had passed. More than 800 men died in the attack, and Father O'Callahan was needed to officiate at the burials.

Finally, the ordeal over, the *Franklin*'s Commanding Officer said Father O'Callahan was "the bravest man I've ever seen in my life." In January 1946, President Truman presented Father O'Callahan with the Medal of Honor, making him the first chaplain ever to receive the nation's highest award for gallantry.

Father O'Callahan was promoted Commander in July 1945 and served aboard the aircraft carrier USS *Franklin D. Roosevelt* until late 1946, when he left active duty to return to his prewar professorship of Mathematics at Holy Cross College. He was promoted to Captain upon his retirement from the Naval Reserve in 1953. Father O'Callahan died in Worcester, Massachusetts, in 1964. In 1968 a destroyer escort,

Alternating between fire fighting and ministering to the wounded and dying, Father O'Callahan spent the day and the following night on duty. Here he gives last rites to crewman Robert C. Blanchard on the flight deck. Even after the fires were under control and the ship stabilized, Father O'Callahan could not rest; there were still 800 men of the ship's complement to be buried. The *Franklin* survived, however, and became the most heavily damaged ship ever to remain afloat. (US Navy)

the USS *O'Callahan*, DE-1051, was commissioned to bear his name.

Private First Class Albert Earnest Schwab, USMCR

Okinawa was the next island in the leap-frog of US forces in the Pacific theater. An island 60 miles long and between 2 and 18 miles in width, the island's long axis runs roughly north/south. The invasion began on April 1, 1945, at a point on the west coast somewhat south of the center of the island.

American forces chosen for the invasion consisted of the US Army XXIV Corps (7th and 96th Infantry Divisions, with the 27th and 77th Divisions in reserve) and the III Marine Amphibious Corps (1st and 6th Marine Divisions with the 2nd Marine division as reserve): in all 184,000 troops were available for the assault. Private First Class Albert E. Schwab was one of this force, attached to the headquarters company of the first battalion of the 5th Marines of the veteran 1st Marine Division.

US troops met no opposition upon landing and according to plan, the Army divisions turned south while the Marines wheeled to the north. Resistance increased as the men pushed inland where the Japanese were concentrated. The savage fighting intensified as the Americans moved further inland and discovered the Japanese defenders firmly positioned in a series of defensive lines constructed of pillboxes, trenches, underground tunnels, and bunkers. The 6th Marine Division pushed east and took the airbase at Yontan and then proceeded northeast 20 miles until they were held up by

Faced with a variety of difficulties crossing the coral reefs of South Seas islands, the US produced a series of amphibious tractors called "Amtracs" by the troops. Here a line of Marines from the 6th Division marches past a disabled vehicle on Okinawa. (NARA)

the Motobu defense system on April 12. The 1st Division remained further south fighting guerrilla-type actions against the Japanese in the mountains of the Ishikawa Isthmus.

Private First Class Schwab, a 23-year-old former oil worker from Tulsa, Oklahoma, was attached to the 1st Battalion of the 5th Marine Regiment as a flame thrower operator, armed with a portable M-2 backpack flame thrower. Men armed with flame throwers were responsible for clearing out Japanese strong points that impeded the advance of their units, but the range of the M-2 flame thrower was so short that it had to be brought within pistol range of a target before firing. In order to give the flame thrower operator some protection for his close-in work, covering fire was provided by a support team, typically composed of 12 men armed with an assortment of M-1 and automatic rifles, as well as a fuel bearer/alternate operator.

On May 7, the 1st Battalion of the 5th Marines attacked enemy positions in and around Nan Hill. Here the Japanese defenders made a stand that impeded the American attack for 48 hours. As Pfc. Schwab's company advanced against the enemy positions, they came under accurate fire by a Japanese machine gun. Pfc. Schwab, recognizing the danger that the company was in, attempted to outflank the Japanese position, but the further he moved down the line, the more treacherous the terrain became. Finally, Pfc. Schwab's path was completely blocked by a steep stone escarpment. Unwilling to retrace his steps, Pfc. Schwab instead left cover and charged the Japanese machine gun position, even though he had only enough fuel remaining for a 10 second burst of flame. Climbing up the steep slope in the teeth of Japanese machine gun fire and mortar rounds, Pfc. Schwab held his fire until the last possible minute. With a final burst of speed, he reached the Japanese and unleashed a blast of flame that neutralized the position. The rest of his company, heartened by the single-handed heroics of Pfc. Schwab, rose up from cover and took the crest of the ridge.

The moment of victory was fleeting, however, as the Marines immediately came under fire from a second machine gun and a mortar battery positioned on the far slope of the ridge. Pfc. Schwab did not hesitate, but advanced alone against this second threat, even though now desperately low on fuel. With mortar shells bursting on all sides, Pfc. Schwab advanced against the second machine gun as bullets kicked up dust at his feet. Pfc. Schwab closed and fired on the Japanese position, even as he was mortally wounded by fire from the machine gun. With his last strength, Pfc. Schwab once more fired his flame thrower, destroying the machine gun emplacement and allowing his comrades to secure the ridge.

After the war, on Memorial Day, 1946, Pfc. Schwab's Medal of Honor was presented to his three-year-old son in Tulsa, Oklahoma, by the Commander of Naval Air Basic Training Command, Corpus Christi, Texas. In 1949, Pfc. Schwab's body was returned to the US and re-interred in his hometown of Tulsa. Ten years later, a Marine Corps training camp on Okinawa was named in honor of this brave Marine.

Private First Class Albert Schwab is pictured in this official USMC photograph in his green wool service dress uniform that would commonly be worn on walking out occasions in the States but was too warm for most of the Marines' Liberty ports in the Pacific theater. Pfc. Schwab's decoration in the photograph is the Marine marksman's badge. (USMC)

Marines on Okinawa faced a series of natural and man-made strongholds that the Japanese had turned into virtual fortresses. This Marine team takes position around the mouth of a cave near Naha on Okinawa. The Marines have just lobbed a smoke grenade into the cave and are ready to deliver fire should any Japanese defenders still be inside. Combat support teams like this one varied in numbers and composition and were designed to get flame throwers, which had the range of a handgun, into the best position for maximum effectiveness. (Official Navy photograph)

BIBLIOGRAPHY

DeRose, James F. *Unrestricted Warfare: How a New Breed of Officers Led the Submarine Force to Victory in World War II*, John Wiley & Sons Inc. (New York, 2000)

Hammel, Eric. *Aces Against Japan: The American Aces Speak*. Volume I, Pacifica Press (Pacifica, 1992)

Hammel, Eric. *Aces Against Japan II: The American Aces Speak*. Volume III, Pacifica Press (Pacifica, 1996)

Henry, Mark R. Men-at-Arms 342: *The US Army in World War II (I) The Pacific*, Osprey Publishing (Oxford, 2000)

Henry, Mark R. Elite 80: *The US Navy in World War II*, Osprey Publishing (Oxford, 2002)

Holmes, Harry. *The Last Patrol*, The Naval Institute Press (Annapolis, 2001)

Lundstrom, John B. *The First Team: Pacific Naval Air Combat from Pearl Harbor to Midway*, The Naval Institute Press (Annapolis, 1984)

Lundstrom, John B. *The First Team and the Guadalcanal Campaign: Naval Fighter Combat from August to November 1942*, The Naval Institute Press (Annapolis, 1994)

Smurthwaite, David. *The Pacific War Atlas 1941–1945*, Facts On File (New York, 1995)

Thomas, Lowell. *These Men Shall Never Die*, The John C. Winston Company (Philadelphia, 1943)

THE PLATES

A: Chief Water Tender Peter Tomich

Riding at anchor on the northeast side of Ford Island early on the morning of Sunday December 7, 1941, was USS *Utah* (AG-16), an old "Florida" class battleship that had been converted into a target ship by the Navy. Ironically, American aviators had used AG-16 in the weeks preceding the Japanese raid at Pearl Harbor as a target for their practice bombs.

Chief Water Tender Peter Tomich was an immigrant born in Herzegovian, a part of the Austro-Hungarian Empire. By 1941, he was already a veteran of both the Army in World War I as well as 20 years of regular naval service. As a chief water tender, Tomich had the responsibility of maintaining the boilers and steam lines for the power plant of the *Utah*.

Early in the attack, torpedoes launched from the Japanese planes slammed into the side of the *Utah*. As water rushed into the engineering spaces Chief Tomich calmly ordered his crew to safety as he began the process that would keep the boilers of the *Utah* from exploding. When the list of the ship reached 40 degrees, Tomich certainly knew that the ship was doomed, yet he remained at his post and completed his task. Finally at 0812 USS *Utah* capsized taking Chief Water Tender Peter Tomich and 58 of his fellow shipmates to their deaths.

B: Commander Cassin Young; USS *Vestal*, Pearl Harbor, December 7, 1941

Commander Cassin Young was a career Navy officer who graduated from the Naval Academy in 1916, just in time for World War I. He served aboard the USS *Connecticut* (BB-18), assigned training duties along the Atlantic coast during the course of the war. Following the war, he qualified in submarines and commanded the two R class submarines R-23 and R-2, eventually rising to the rank of commander in 1937.

Sunday mornings were full-dress affairs in the prewar US Navy, and on stations like Pearl Harbor, both ship's company and officers alike were dressed in tropical white uniforms for the raising of the colors. Commander Young's uniform is the US Navy dress white uniform with five gold buttons down the front and black shoulder boards that have three gold stripes. Cdr Young is hatless and ribbonless, and his uniform is wet from the sea and damaged from oil because a Japanese bomb blast threw him overboard.

C: Commander Richard Antrim; Makassar, April 1942

Commander Antrim was the most senior of the 150 survivors of the USS *Pope* which had been sunk by the Japanese after the Battle of the Java Sea. It was his responsibility to see to the welfare of the surviving crew members of the USS *Pope*, even in the terrible conditions of a Japanese prison camp. Among Cdr Antrim's other awards are the Navy Cross, won for his bravery during the battles of Makassar and Badoeng Straits and the Bronze Star for meritorious service while a POW. Little is known about Cdr Antrim's uniform, or lack thereof, during captivity, so what is shown is a typical navy uniform of the period. It consists of the khaki long-sleeved shirt, trousers, and black leather oxford shoes.

D: First Lieutenant Jefferson DeBlanc, VMF-112, 1942

First Lieutenant DeBlanc is shown posed in front of his fighter, an F4F-4 Grumman Wildcat. The Wildcat was the mainstay of both the Navy and Marine Corps fighter squadrons during the first two years of the war and bore the brunt of the Japanese air attacks at Henderson Field on Guadalcanal. The strong points of the Grumman were a battery of four .50-cal. machine guns (six in later variants), self-sealing fuel tanks, and cockpit armor for the pilot, which allowed the Wildcat to take tremendous punishment in a fight and still remain an effective aircraft. This particular

With little food and savage discipline, the conditions in Japanese prison camps were abominable. Not a signatory to the Geneva Convention, Japan adhered to its Bushido tradition, which viewed surrender as dishonorable, and accordingly, viewed prisoners of war as men beyond contempt, to be kept alive only for the work they could perform. Thus, virtually no provision was made for prisoner welfare. Here prisoners are made to march to a new camp to keep them from falling into the hands of the advancing Allied armies; more or less able-bodied prisoners carry their own sick and wounded in makeshift litters. (NARA)

fighter is painted in a scheme used at the Battle of Midway in 1942, of blue-gray on the upper surfaces and light gray on the undersides of the craft. The national insignia of a blue circle and white star would appear on both sides of the fuselage and both the upper and lower wing surfaces. Lt. DeBlanc mentions in his memoirs that the particular fighter he was flying the day he won the Medal of Honor was not his usual plane, but was painted with a "Blond Bombshell" and the name *Impatient Virgin* on the engine cowling.

Lt. DeBlanc is shown wearing the AN-S-31 standard flight suit, M450 style flight helmet and the AN standard "Mae West" life jacket. Both the helmet and flight suit are made from light cotton twill material.

Among the unsung heroes of World War II were the men responsible for the maintenance of the aircraft. Located on remote bases, such as Henderson Field, the ground crews had the difficult job of keeping the "Cactus Air Force" in the sky. Plagued by supply problems of all kinds, the ground crews often had to scavenge parts from damaged planes just to keep the squadrons in the air. This crew chief, to Lt. DeBlanc's right, wears the standard issue USMC combat and fatigue uniform consisting of a one-piece coverall and

cap made of herringbone twill cotton material. The uniform has USMC and the EGA insignia stenciled on the left breast pocket and a smaller EGA on the front of the fatigue hat (all obscured here).

E: Commander Richard O'Kane; USS *Tang*, October 24, 1944

After World War I, the US Navy embarked upon producing a submarine that could take on silent advanced scouting operations ahead of the main battle line of warships. This concept came to be called the "fleet" boat. The USS Tang (SS-306) was one such vessel, being part of the new "Balao" class of submarines. The Tang was 311ft long and displaced 2,400 tons while submerged. Her four 1600 horsepower diesel engines powered her through the water at 22 knots and her four electric engines would allow her to run at speeds of 9 knots while submerged. The submarine's armament consisted of one 5in. deck gun, one 40mm Bofors gun, one 20mm Oerlikon, and several .50-cal. machine guns that could be mounted at various stations on the deck. For her primary mission of sinking enemy ships, the USS *Tang* would rely on ten 21in. torpedo tubes, six in the bow and

On May 1, 1944, off Truk Lagoon, the USS *Tang,* as part of a lifeguard mission, rescued 22 aircrew men, including these nine men stranded on a Navy "Kingfisher" off the USS *North Carolina.* (US Navy)

USS *Tang* (SS-306) was a "Balao" class fleet submarine, 311ft in length, displacing 2,400 tons submerged with a crew complement of one captain, seven officers, eight CPOs, and 54 crew members. This official naval photograph was taken on December 2, 1943, off Mare Island, California, following her refit. (US Navy)

A Navy corpsman attached to the Marines, Hospital Corpsman Apprentice Robert Eugene Bush received the Medal of Honor. Bush combined armed combat with life saving, a necessity brought about by the Japanese practice of treating medical personnel as combatants. Red Cross insignia were favored Japanese targets. In addition to medals and bond drives, America celebrated her combat heroes in many ways. One unique way was found by the *Navy Times* service newspaper, in the comic strip shown here. (US Navy)

four in the stern, carrying 24 Mk. XV torpedoes on her war patrol.

The conning tower design on American fleet boats underwent a variety of changes during the course of the war, with many of the earliest "Gato" class boats having a nearly enclosed cabin for the officer of the watch at the head of the conning tower. The vulnerability of submarines to air attack caused designers to cut back the fairwater (the front edge of the conning tower) and lower it, in order to make a platform for additional anti-aircraft protection. The new position, from which an officer conned the vessel, was located now above this 20mm gun position at the base of the periscope shears closer to the conning tower hatch. Commander O'Kane was in charge of the USS *Tang* from the bridge on the night of the surface attack on the Japanese convoy. As is tradition, Cdr O'Kane, after giving the order to dive the boat, would be the last officer on deck with the responsibility to close the main hatch.

While on the surface, the commander of the sub had full control of the vessel by a variety of devices to communicate to the crew below decks. The device to Cdr O'Kane's right is the Target Bearing Transmitter, or TBT, used in the aiming of torpedoes. While in service, the

TBT communicated directly with the torpedo officer who fed the information into the Torpedo Data Computer, a mechanical device that figured the correct firing solutions automatically.

As the war progressed and American radar became more reliable, night surface actions by US Navy submarines became more common. One tactic favored by aggressive commanders like O'Kane was to spot the convoy by means of the periscope, then surface to commence an "end around" or high speed surface run in order to get in front of the convoy, and fire as they passed. The low silhouette of the submarine while on the surface made discovery by Japanese vessels extremely unlikely unless they were also equipped with the latest radar.

F: Hospital Apprentice 1st Class Robert Eugene Bush; Okinawa, May 2, 1945

Just as the Marine Corps relied upon the Navy for transport, they also relied upon the Navy's Hospital Corps for medical care. Navy corpsmen acted as battlefield medics. Wherever the Marines fought, Navy corpsmen were there. One of these was 19-year-old Hospital Apprentice 1st Class Robert Eugene Bush.

On May 2, 1945, he was assigned to a rifle company of the 5th Marines during the invasion of Okinawa. That day, the 5th Marines were pushing uphill towards a ridge against determined Japanese resistance. The slope was strewn with Marine casualties, and Corpsman Bush moved unceasingly among them rendering aid despite the withering fire all around him. When the attack passed over the crest of the ridge, he moved up to the top of the slope to aid a wounded Marine officer. A Japanese counterattack swept over the ridge just as he began administering blood plasma to his patient. As the Japanese approached, Corpsman Bush gallantly held up the plasma bottle with one hand and fired a pistol at the Japanese with the other. Then he grabbed a carbine and killed six advancing Japanese. He suffered several serious wounds himself, including the loss of an eye. He remained guarding his "officer patient" until the enemy were repulsed. Then, according to the official citation, he "valiantly refus[ed] medical treatment for himself until his officer patient had been evacuated ..."

A recent Navy publication tells a slightly different story. Once Corpsman Bush reached the unconscious wounded officer, he began to administer plasma. Suddenly the officer regained consciousness, jumped up, and ran back down the hill with the plasma bottle trailing behind him. Corpsman Bush was left alone in his exposed forward position when the Japanese counterattacked. In a very tough position, he had only his pistol and the officer's discarded carbine to defend himself. He held off the Japanese for a while, until they began to throw grenades, wounding Corpsman Bush in the eye, shoulder, buttocks, and stomach. With death imminent, Corpsman Bush left his shelter and managed to move to his left and up the hill. The Japanese did not see his move and continued to bombard the shell hole he had just left.

Corpsman Bush found an M-1 rifle as he crawled up the slope and soon found himself above and behind the Japanese. Somehow, despite his wounds, he attacked the Japanese from the rear and routed them. After this, he managed to make his way back to the Marine lines alone.

G: Boatswain's Mate 2nd Class Owen Francis Hammerberg; Pearl Harbor, February 17, 1945

On May 21, 1944, while an LST was engaged in the routine loading of ammunition in the West Loch of Pearl Harbor, some of the munitions detonated aboard the LST causing a vast explosion. In the space of a few moments, five LSTs (numbers 43, 69, 179, 353, and 480) were destroyed and some 559 men were killed or wounded by the explosion. The destruction of these vessels not only hampered the supply of the Saipan invasion effort, but also was a hazard to safe navigation in the shallow waters of Pearl Harbor. Therefore, the Navy began salvage efforts to remove the sunken vessels.

On February 17, 1945, during normal salvage operations in one of the sunken LSTs, an accident occurred. Two Navy divers who had been working within the hulk of the LST, tunneling in the mud with jet nozzles, became trapped beneath the surface of the water when a cave-in occurred. Boatswain's Mate 2nd Class Owen Hammerberg immediately began a dive in order to rescue his fellow divers. Using the jet nozzle in the murky water, Hammerberg was able to wash a passage to the original excavation where he found the first diver. Freeing his comrade from the twisted steel that entrapped him, Boatswain's Mate Hammerberg continued searching for the other diver, who was trapped deeper in the wreck. Working alone in near pitch-blackness in a twisted maze of steel which threatened his own air lines and with total disregard for his own safety, Boatswain's Mate Hammerberg used his jet nozzle to reach the lost diver. Unfortunately, the action of the jet nozzle caused another cave-in, which trapped Boatswain's Mate Hammerberg beneath a piece of heavy steel that pinned him above the trapped diver. The weight of the metal on his chest killed Hammerberg, but his

The fight for Iwo Jima was extremely heavy, and so were the casualties. This aid station on the beach just behind the front lines, is staffed by US Navy Corpsmen attached to Marine ground units. The Corpsmen are giving whole blood transfusions. They were trained to insert needles into the inside of the elbow because it offers a large, easily found vein. Of interest are the arm boards which the corpsmen have attached to their patients: the boards were necessary to stop the wounded from accidentally pulling out the needles or bending their arms, which would cut off the flow of blood. (Official Navy Photograph)

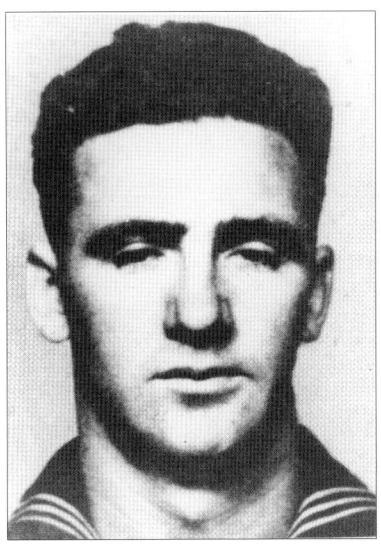

This official Navy Photograph is the only know image of Boatswain's Mate 2nd class Owen Francis Hammerberg. During World War II, Boatswain's Mate Hammerberg received the Medal of Honor for non-combat experiences. (US Navy)

death saved the life of his shipmate who was rescued from the cave-in.

Significantly, Hammerberg's posthumous award of the Medal of Honor marked the final time in the history of the US Navy that the Medal was awarded for humanitarian, rather than action in the face of the enemy.

Hammerberg is wearing the US Navy's Mk. V diving equipment that consists of the Mk. V dive helmet (also known as a bonnet), a heavy canvas dive suit, weighted leather belt, heavy dive boots with weighted soles, and a Morse dive knife. This venerable suit had its inception in 1912 when Gunner's Mate S. D. Stillson began the US testing of the diving tables established by the British Royal Navy earlier in the century. From the data gathered by these dives, the Morse and Schrader Company was able to design the Mk. V gear, which went into service in 1916 and remained in the Navy inventory until the early 1980s. The Mk. V was designed to serve the dual purposes of both salvage and repair operations; however, the major limitation of the gear was the umbilical air line that attached the diver to the ship and restricted his motions with the constant danger of becoming caught on underwater obstructions.

Perhaps the most spectacular use of the Mk. V equipment came in 1939 when it was used by Navy divers to rescue 33 members of the crew of USS *Squalus*, SS-192, which had sunk in 325ft of water off the New Hampshire coast. Four US Navy divers, William Badders, Orson Crandal, James H. MacDonald, and John Milhaloski, received the Medal of Honor in the operation that rescued the majority of the *Squalus* crew. Ironically, John Milhaloski was one of the divers that participated in the salvage operation of the six LSTs that sank in the West Loch

of Pearl Harbor where Hammerberg died. The USS *Hammerberg*, DE-1015, a destroyer escort, was named in memorial to the heroic diver and served in the US Navy from 1955 to 1974.

H: Sergeant "Manila" John Basilone; Lunga Ridge, Guadalcanal, October, 1942

Sergeant John Basilone was in charge of a squad of heavy machine guns defending a section of Lunga Ridge. His squad, like other Marine outfits on Guadalcanal, was armed with the Browning M1917A1 .30-cal. water-cooled machine gun. The Browning was a rugged design (weighing 93lbs) that had been introduced to the US forces in 1917, just in time to be used in World War I. Eventually, the water-cooled variant would be replaced with the M1919A4 air-cooled version of the weapon. The M1917 had the capacity to fire 600 rounds per minute with an effective range of 1,800 yards.

Sgt. Basilone is wearing the standard issue combat uniform for Marine ground units early in the war. This uniform consists of a light OD colored shirt and trousers made from cotton herringbone twill material. Stenciled on the left breast pocket in black is the Marine Corps insignia of an Eagle, Globe, and Anchor with the letters USMC above it. The sergeant's personal gear at the time of the fight was an M1927 pattern pistol belt, first-aid pouch, ammo case, and a brown leather holster for his .45-cal. Colt automatic pistol. By 1942, the old M1917 "Tin Hat" had been replaced by the M2 style steel pot helmet familiar to modern movie-going audiences. Lastly, a pair of russet leather rough-out ankle boots and a pair of tan canvas gaiters, into which the trouser legs were tucked, completed the uniform.

Sergeant Basilone was in charge of a squad of .30-cal. water-cooled machine guns similar to the one shown in this early war-training photograph. With the water-cooling jacket, the M1917 Browning had a higher rate of sustained fire than the more familiar air-cooled M1919 version, making it a favorite for troops in defensive positions. (NARA)

INDEX

References to illustrations are shown in **bold**. Plates are shown with page and caption locators in brackets.